Joyful Ways to Teach Young Children to Write Poetry

BY JODI WEISBART

SCHOLASTIC
PROFESSIONAL BOOKS

NEW YORK • TORONTO • LONDON • AUCKLAND • SYDNEY
MEXICO CITY • NEW DELHI • HONG KONG • BUENOS AIRES

To Mom, Dad, Michael, and Kevin

for all of your love and support.

ACKNOWLEDGMENTS

A special thanks to Hindy List, without whom this book would never have happened. I am also appreciative of all of my colleagues, students, and their families at P.S. 3: my colleagues, for all of their support, interest, and willingness to try teaching poetry in their rooms; my students, for all of their incredible and inspiring words and work; and their families, for their interest and continual support. Thank you to Elena Davis for being a wonderful cooperating teacher and sharing her joy of teaching with me, and to Pam Mayer for her wonderful songs, poems, and management tips.

I am also most appreciative of my editors, Wendy Murray and Joanna Davis-Swing, who made writing my first book such an enjoyable experience. Finally, to all of my friends and family whose genuine pride and interest in this project began with its conception and never ceased, thank you.

Page 45, "Riding on the Train" by Eloise Greenfield from *Honey I Love* by Eloise Greenfield. Text copyright © 1978 by Eloise Greenfield. Used by permission of HarperCollins Publishers.

Page 62, "This Tooth" by Lee Bennett Hopkins. Copyright © 1970 by Lee Bennett Hopkins. Reprinted by permission of Curtis Brown Ltd.

Page 64, "Our Washing Machine" by Patricia Hubbell from *The Apple Vendor's Fair* by Patricia Hubbell. Copyright © 1963, 1991 by Patricia Hubbel. Reprinted by permission of Marian Reiner.

Page 66, "Good Books, Good Times" by Lee Bennett Hopkins. Copyright © 1985, 1995 by Lee Bennett Hopkins. Reprinted by permission of Curtis Brown Ltd.

Page 79, "Nature is Very Busy" by Frances Gorman Risser from *Perfect Poems for Teaching Phonics*. Reprinted by permission of Scholastic Inc.

▲▲▲▲▲▲▲▲▲▲▲▲▲

Front cover and interior design by Kathy Massaro
Cover and interior photographs on pages 5, 6, 20, 28, 36, 44, 54, 64, 72, and 79 by Nina Roberts.
All others courtesy of author.

ISBN 0-439-22243-5
Copyright © 2001 by Jodi Weisbart
All rights reserved.
Printed in U.S.A.

CONTENTS

PREFACE

▲▲▲▲▲▲▲▲▲▲▲▲▲▲

WHEN I WAS IN THE FOURTH GRADE, my teacher, Mrs. Corman, put Beethoven's *Moonlight Sonata* on the phonograph and invited us to write the images that came to mind as we listened to the music. I remember writing a simple poem about a sleeping boy, his face illuminated by the beams of moonlight coming through the window as he slept. I don't remember much more about the poem, but I do remember my thrill when I was asked to read my poem aloud to the entire school.

I never forgot that experience or the encouragement Mrs. Corman provided for me to write poetry.

When I see the joyful children in Jodi Weisbart's classroom reading and chanting poetry, writing their own poems, and publishing and celebrating their writing, I know that long after they leave Jodi's class, their memories of these experiences will remain with them as mine did. For those of us who have visited Jodi and worked alongside her, her teaching seems magical; but there is method to her "magic."

Jodi believes in the power of poetry and that we all have poetry inside of us. In *Joyful Ways to Teach Young Children to Write Poetry* Jodi shares it all with us. In these practical and well thought-out chapters, Jodi describes her year-long writing plan and her step-by-step approach to bringing children and poetry together.

For those of us who lack confidence about teaching poetry to young children, this book is a godsend. As a staff developer, I will be using it as a guide and sharing it with the teachers I work with. I strongly recommend it to anyone who wants to bring the power of poetry to his or her students. It is a book to celebrate.

Hindy List

DISTRICT 2 WRITING STAFF DEVELOPER
NEW YORK CITY PUBLIC SCHOOLS

When I first thought about teaching poetry to my kindergarten class, it seemed like a silly idea. How in the world would kindergarten students who were barely writing be able to write poetry? But then I thought, that's just it—this is what they need to push them with their writing and get them to write more. So I jumped in with both feet, and so did my students. I thought I would challenge them with a poetry unit and see if my hypothesis worked—if having them write poems would motivate them to write more. It did.

I have high expectations for my students in every part of the day, for every academic and nonacademic area we work on together. I often dream up ambitious projects for my students and their families, and then wonder if I've asked too much of them. However, I am never disappointed. The children rise to the occasion, and I am always impressed that, no matter how high the bar is set, the students succeed. I seek to provide them with as much support, caring, loving, and good humor as they need to find that success. We create a community of peer teachers in our classroom, working together toward our goals. My philosophy, in a nutshell, is to work hard together, play hard together, and celebrate together often.

Therefore, when I envisioned starting the poetry genre study with my class, I dreamed big. I organized the poetry unit around a variety of forms, such as list poems, sound poems, and repeating poems. I introduced each topic with a mini-lesson followed by independent writing time and a whole-class share session. I tried to keep my mini-lessons brief and open-ended. Even though I was introducing a new idea or skill, I didn't want the children to feel intimidated by it. Rather, I wanted to throw it out there and give them the chance to explore it on their own. Their work proved to me that they needed no further explanations.

Before beginning our poetry genre study we had established our writer's workshop routines and explored other genres of writing. Our daily writing workshop and other year-long routines, such as the shared reading of weekly poems, helped to lay the foundation for our poetry genre study. In this book, I share our story of becoming poets.

CHAPTER 1

Writing Workshop in Kindergarten

From the first day of kindergarten I tell my students that they are all writers. Declan raises his hand and exclaims, "I don't know how to write!" To him, writing is meant to be with letters and words, things he doesn't know yet. I want to expand his definition to include any story told on paper. I ask Declan, "Do you draw pictures?"

"Yes," he says hesitantly.

"Then you are a writer!"

Knowing that it will take more than these words of encouragement to persuade him, I start to model for all my students what writing can be. I start by writing stories about myself because that's what I know best. I tell my students that they can write about themselves, too. I model drawing a picture of my family. While I draw the picture I tell them, "This is my family. This is my mom, Barbara; my dad, Steve; and my brother, Michael. We are at my house. I wrote a story about the people in my family." At this point I do not add letters or words. I leave it as a story written as a picture. Children begin to understand that pictures tell stories, and soon they are off to write their own stories with pictures.

The first story I share with my students.

Setup for Success

Before starting my writing workshop, I organize my classroom in a way that will support independent writers. As a novice teacher I struggled with classroom organization. My students sported writing folders crammed with crumpled and ripped papers; some work mysteriously landed under tables or in the block area. I noticed that every time I handed out the writing folders, my students had to wait a long time before I was done. My routine was certainly not calming, and the atmosphere it created was not conducive to thoughtful and creative writing. My principal, Sheri Donovan, and staff developer, Hindy List, made some helpful suggestions that transformed my writing workshop.

Writing Folders

Now, my preparation for a successful writing workshop begins before students arrive in the fall. During the summer, I buy an assortment of colored two-pocket folders. I usually buy five or six folders in each of five colors (red, yellow, green, blue, purple) so five or six students can be in a writing group sharing the same-colored folders. During the first few days of school, I encourage students to write or tell stories about themselves in any way they know. I confer with each child as she writes or talks about these initial stories, so I can assess the writing abilities of every student in my

Writing Center

Our writing center is the central location for our classroom writing materials. I usually use the top of a bookcase and one of its shelves to house everything we need. I store the writing folders there, along with different kinds of paper (appropriate to the unit of study), pens, pencils, markers, and crayons.

The folders, marker containers, and crayon boxes are color-coded for each writing group.

class. I use the information I gather from these conferences to create heterogeneous writing groups, where students can see one another as writing teachers. I want students to turn to each other, as well as to me, for inspiration and writing help.

I use the writing groups primarily as a management tool. I code magazine holders and crayon and marker containers with the folder colors. Each writing group then is responsible for getting its own folders (stored in the color-coded magazine holders) and markers and cleaning them up when writing time is over.

After assigning the students to writing groups, I introduce and explain how to use the writing folders by saying something like this:

> "Today I'm going to give you your very own writing folder to keep all of your writing in. This will be a place for you to keep your writing so that you can work on it for more than one day. Each of you has a folder with a special color. All children with the same color folder will work together as a writing group. Your writing group will share markers, crayons, and pencils and help each other with your writing. Today, when writing time is over, please make sure that you put your writing neatly in your folder and that your folders and markers get put back at the writing center."

I model placing a paper neatly in my folder. Then, I have one group slowly model how to get their folders and markers and get ready to work. In the beginning of the year I usually assign one person in the group to get the folders and another to get the markers. Those same students are responsible for putting the materials away. During the first week of this routine we go very slowly. One group gets the materials and the rest of us watch. I say, "Green group will work at the long low table in the back today. Julia, please get the folders. Isa, please get the markers. The rest of the green group, please meet them at the back table." This routine is introduced after the children have already been writing informally, without folders, for a few days.

Writing Center Materials

In the beginning of the year, I limit the materials in the writing center. Later I will supply more paper options and markers, but, initially, I want the students to get organized with a simple set of materials. I find that the more slowly I introduce the materials, the more likely it is that they will be treated gently. Therefore, initially I put out:

- Plain 8 1/2" x 11" white paper
- Crayons
- Pencils

I introduce how to use markers only after the students become comfortable with getting and putting away their writing folders. I am very specific in my instructions on using markers. We talk about using markers only on our papers, not on each other. We talk about how to make sure the markers are capped, and together we listen for the "snap of the cap" as I close several markers. I have students show us how to listen for the "snap of the cap." I make students the "marker police." It sounds silly, but I've found that this deliberate attention to the smallest details helps my students become responsible for the materials they use. This five-minute discussion on taking care of our markers makes the difference between needing ten marker sets for the year or 30.

Later in the year, as we move toward writing poems and longer pieces, including books, I add different kinds of paper to our writing center. I also show students how to fold the paper to make books. Modeling is crucial. Otherwise, students end up unintentionally wasting lots of materials. As students begin to write more, I also add "writing pens" to our writing center. Students use special "writing pens" (I use PaperMate™ black and blue felt tip pens) when adding their words to their drawings. I find that ink shows up more easily on their drawings than does pencil.

Writing Workshop

I structure my daily writing workshop into three sections: the mini-lesson, independent writing time, and the class share. This structure is taken from the Writing Project at Columbia University Teachers College. Early in the year I take the time to show students my expectations. I model the way I'd like them to sit for a mini-lesson. I have the class scoot close to me at my easel and sit pretzel-legged on the rug. I wait for their eyes and bodies to be still and tell me that they are ready to listen. I also model the way to get started writing: I show them how to get their folders, choose paper, and find a spot to work in. Finally, I model how to respond to each other during share time. As one child shares his work, I offer comments or suggestions that might be appropriate.

"Kevin, I like the way you used a lot of colors in your writing. You really included a lot of details in your story."

　　　Or

"Liana, you wrote a lot of words today. Where did you look for help with those words?"

　　　Or

"Elijah, you started writing about a trip with your family to the beach. What did you do at the beach? Were you there for a day, a few days, a week? Is that something you think that you might want to add tomorrow?"

During the first few weeks of school, I spend more time on the routines around writing and setting up my expectations for their behavior, than on the actual writing. This time invested early in the year helps ensure that our actual writing time for the rest of the year will be as productive as possible.

The amount of time we spend during writing workshop (mini-lesson, writing time, share) lengthens throughout the year. In the beginning of the year our writing workshop is broken down this way:

5 minutes	**Mini-Lesson**
20 minutes	**Independent Writing Time**
5–10 minutes	**Share**
30–35 minutes total	

As the year progresses, both our writing time and share time lengthen. By the end of the year, students may be working on their writing independently for 40 minutes. The total writing workshop time at that point is 50–60 minutes.

Mini-Lesson

Lucy Calkins, in her book, *The Art of Teaching Writing* says, "…most of the K–6 teachers…begin their workshops with a four or five minute mini-lesson. After talking to the children or giving them tips about good writing, the teacher sends them off to draft, revise, and confer with each other."

I, too, start my workshops with mini-lessons. I gather my students on the rug and offer them a story, a thought, or a noticing. These mini-lessons are the crux of the writing workshop. Early in the year mini-lessons are little bits of information, ideas on how to get started, or suggestions for writing topics. As the year progresses, the mini-lessons grow out of the work students are doing.

In conferences with students, I assess their work and the ways in which they respond to my mini-lessons. I take anecdotal notes and use my assessments as the foundation of future mini-lessons. Often student work itself will serve as a mini-lesson. For my students, mini-lessons are suggestions and ideas. I want my students to write about their own ideas and to write in a way that they feel comfortable. If my mini-lesson gives them an idea or a form for writing down their ideas, that is wonderful. But, if not—if that day they aren't inspired by my mini-lesson—that's okay, too.

My mini-lessons range in content from generating ideas to writing down initial sounds to folding books and using staplers. Mini-lessons will vary from teacher to teacher, from class to class, and from year to year. The key to making them successful is using your students' ideas, writing, and work behaviors as a springboard for topics. Perhaps one day I'll notice that Emily is writing but not leaving spaces between words. The next day I'll do a mini-lesson for everyone on leaving spaces between words. Similarly, if I notice that Agim is having trouble getting his ideas down in writing, the next day we'll have a mini-lesson on what to do when that happens. I might say,

> Yesterday during writing time, I noticed that some of you were having trouble getting started. I also noticed that some of you got to work right away. I was wondering if you had some ideas about what to do when you are having trouble getting started.

This becomes the day's mini-lesson: A five-minute class-generated discussion of what to do. We share ideas, and then I send the students off to write. I may model writing a story of my own, incorporating the suggestions the students offer. I try, however, to keep the mini-lesson truly "mini."

Independent Writing Time

Following the mini-lesson, I send students off to work independently in their writing groups. It's a time for students to delve into their own realities and express, through pictures or words, what is important to them. Through our mini-lessons during the year, children are introduced to various genres of writing. As they dabble in these genres, their writing grows.

During independent writing time, I confer with individual children. In the beginning of the year I establish the expectation that I will not always be available to help during writing time. I teach children to use the members of their writing groups as "teachers" and to ask them for help. Setting up this expectation allows me to spend a few quality moments with individual children during writing time.

As I move about the room I notice the work that the students are doing. Through these observations and conferences, I assess the work going on in the classroom and get ideas for future mini-lessons. In addition, I watch for students who are working fastidiously, trying something new, or tackling an idea that was mentioned during the mini-lesson. These are the students I may ask to share during our daily share session.

Share

At the end of independent writing time, we clean up our folders, put our crayons, pencils, and markers away, and return to the rug for a "writer's share." The share is not only a celebration of the work we've done, but a way for students to share new strategies they've discovered, new ideas they've written about, and new ways they can help their peers. I choose two to four students to share each day.

I use a class grid (shown below) to help me keep track of which students I conferred with on a given day and who had an opportunity to share their work with the rest of the class. This grid ensures that I give each child an equal opportunity to share his writing. Of course, there are some students who never want to share their work, and some who always do. I tell my students that I will pick the students who share each day to ensure that everyone gets a turn. It is important to me that I be able to choose who shares, because then I can shape the structure of the share session to focus on a certain idea or strategy. As I confer with students, I ask them if they'd like to share their work. This gives students the opportunity to decline if they want to. If a student declines, I offer to help him share. This usually alleviates any nervousness and leads to an agreement to share the work. I try to encourage even the shyest child to share at least a few times throughout the year.

This grid helps me track who I've conferred with and who has shared over the course of a week. It also gives me a place to record ideas for future mini-lessons.

WRITING SHARE

	MON. 10/2	TUES. 10/3	WED. 10/4	THURS. 10/5	FRI. 10/6	Noticings (Future Mini-lessons)
Alicia	√family	√park			√friends S	
Amanda	√sister		√family	√school		
Bryan	√beach S		√family		√brother	using alphabet chart
Cosmo	√great adventure	√cat		√sister		
Declan	√sick	√sick		√july 4th	√ S	needs work on STRETCHING OUT SOUNDS
Donna		√friends S	√school		√reading	beg/mid/end sounds
Eli	√maine		√maine trip		√maine trip	
Elijah	√family		√sister		√house	word wall + new topics
Emma	√house	√her room		√kitchen S		
Esmir	√skateboard		√house S		√dad	
Fakoya		√ S	√family		√birthday	
Gabrielle	√family S		√school		√trip	maybe ready for picture dictionary
Isadora		√animals S	√pets		√house	using words you can read to help spell.
Joey		√friends S	√friends			
Justin	√family		√mom	√house S		
Liana	√savings			√family		
Lucian	√brighton beach	√surfing		√dad S		
Noah	√family		√ S		√legos	writing runs together SPACING
Rachel	√trip		√trip S		√paris	
Shawnee	√family		√sister		√school	
Sierra		√savings		√family S		
Vinny	√fishing	√hotel		√trip	√hotel S	lower case letters

√ = conference   S = share

Once the authors are chosen, they sit at the front of our meeting area with the rest of the students gathered at their feet. Early in the year, I model reading in a loud voice, sharing pictures, and taking comments and questions from the rest of the class. Creating an enjoyable and effective share time takes the entire year.

My friend, Pam Mayer, a teacher at Manhattan New School, taught me a wonderful management technique that a student teacher of hers had created, "Magic Five." "Magic Five" consists of five behaviors that are conducive to attentive listening:

1. Sit flat on your bottom.
2. Sit with your legs crossed like a pretzel.
3. Keep your mouth closed.
4. Put your hands in your lap.
5. Keep your eyes on the person who is talking.

I introduce the "Magic Five" on the first day of school, and we use it at every class gathering. I teach the students to help each other remember "Magic Five" and to wait for students who are not listening attentively. Therefore, rather than constantly saying, "sit down, stop talking, keep your hands to yourself," I simply say, "I'm waiting for you to be 'Magic Five.'" This simple management technique has been crucial in creating a classroom in which students listen to and celebrate the work that each of us does each day.

Early in the year I ask my student authors questions or make comments about their work, modeling the kinds of talk I expect from students later in the year. I model asking questions like, "Who did you go to the park with?" or "Where were you when that happened?" I ask questions that will encourage the writers to add more detail to their stories. I also model giving praise for the work students did. For example, "I like the way you used so many details in your drawing," or "I like the way you labeled your pictures." In modeling the questions and comments, I provide a structure for students to use in commenting on the work being shared.

After a few weeks of such modeling, I begin to ask for questions, comments, and suggestions from the class. At this point, students begin to become experts not only in enriching their own writing, but also at helping their peers expand their initial ideas. Throughout the year, I empower my students to be writing teachers. I consistently tell them that I am not the only teacher in the room, and I show them how to help one another. By the end of the year I am doing very little probing and letting my little writing teachers take over.

Conferences

Each day I try to check in with every writer in my classroom. I note if they are on task and what they're writing about (see writer's share grid on page 12). Beyond this, I try to have a few in-depth conferences with individual students each day. These writing conferences can last from two to five minutes each. During each conference, I use the "Noticings" section of my share grid to keep track of their writing progress and to gather ideas for future whole-class mini-lessons. This helps me remember what I'm working on with each child from day to day.

Lucy Calkins writes on conferences, "If a conference is going well, the child's energy for writing increases....When content conferences work well, children not only realize that the details about their topic matter, they also learn that in order to write well, they must keep their eye on their subject" (*The Art of Teaching Writing*). I keep these ideas in mind whenever I confer with a student. I always start by asking students to tell me about their writing. I listen and watch as they retell their story. I ask questions about stories—things students may have said but not written about or drawn. I try to focus them on the important details in the story and give them strategies for continuing their work.

Each conference is different, as each child is working in a different way on different ideas. With some of my students we focus on letter sounds and labeling, while with others we focus on developing details. The conference is a time for me to individually connect with each student and assess what he can do and needs to work on. I find I can accomplish a lot in a very short time, as shown in the following conference transcript.

Jodi: Cosmo, tell me what you're writing about today.

Cosmo: I'm writing a story about going to an amusement park with my family. It was fun.

Jodi: I see that you've written about going on the Ferris wheel. What was that like?

Cosmo: I could see everything from the top of the Ferris wheel. I wasn't scared. It was really neat.

Jodi: That's interesting. That sounds like you have more writing to add to your story. Could you write more about being on the Ferris wheel and what that was like?

Cosmo: Yeah, I think I'll add that tomorrow.

In addition, during the conferences I always praise the work being done, help students make a plan for what they're going to do next, and offer a strategy that might be useful in achieving the aforementioned goal.

Inspiration

Typically I start writing workshop with an anecdote about my family or my life. I start my mini-lessons this way because I want my students to recognize that we all have stories to tell—and that many things in our lives can make good stories.

I like to use the word "inspire" in class discussions. Often after telling a story about the park, or the beach, or a vacation, my students will raise their hands and offer their own connections. After returning from a vacation in Hawaii, I told my students some stories about my trip and modeled writing about it for them.

Logan: Hey, I've been to Hawaii. I went to Kauai. I went to the beach.

Jodi: Logan, did I inspire you to write about the beach?

Logan: I'm going to write about that.

Eddie: I go to Virginia Beach with my mom and dad.

Jodi: Logan and I inspired you to write about the beach? Will you write about that today?

Emily: I'm moving to the beach. You inspired me, too!

As the year goes by, children often talk about being inspired by a story or inspiring one another. I love hearing them tell each other that they've been inspired to write about something—when, in fact, it is they who are the true inspirations.

Beginning of the Year Mini-Lessons

For the first month or so of school, my mini-lessons concentrate on how to generate an idea for a story, writing a story with details, and sharing work with others. Each day I focus on modeling a behavior that will help my students feel successful at writing. Here are some mini-lessons for the first month of school:

- Getting our writing materials (folders, markers, crayons, or pencils and paper)
- Generating ideas for writing (What can I write about today?)
- Using details in our pictures
- Planning out the words to write
- Labeling our writing with words or initial sounds
- Revisiting our writing the next day
- Sharing our writing with others
- Asking questions or giving suggestions to other writers
- Using the word wall
- Cleaning up after writing time

Using Details in Our Pictures

Details are important to a story, whether in words or in pictures. During my early mini-lessons I focus mainly on telling a story through pictures. I tell the children true stories about my family and my childhood, and they listen with rapt attention. As I draw, I focus on the details of my picture—the color of my hair and the ribbons in my pigtails, or the clothes that my mom wore. I encourage the children to use details in their drawings to help bring out the story. My colleague Elena taught me to teach the children to pay attention to background and "see-through clothes"—the black-outlined shirts that many children draw without filling them in with color or patterns. She would say, "Where are you? Are you floating in the air?" The student would smile sheepishly and say, "No, we are at the _____," and Elena would encourage her to add that important detail to her story.

This focus on details within the pictures is a fundamental beginning to the success of young writers. It turns a 5-minute piece of writing into a 45-minute or 2-day piece of work. Recognizing the importance of details in writing helps students raise their standards for their own writing.

Labeling

Each day as we continue to work on our writing, I model new techniques for students to try during writing time. After concentrating on using details in our pictures, I encourage students to add words or sounds they know to enhance their stories' meaning.

For example, I take the story that I wrote about my family out of my writing folder (I keep one, too). I look at the pictures and retell the story to the class. "You know, I could add something to this story so that if someone else were reading it, they would know who these people were without my needing to tell them. Does anyone have any ideas about what I could add?" The students usually suggest putting the names of my family members on my story, and so I do. I teach them how to label their drawings. I add "me" next to my picture, and "mom" by the picture of my mom, and so forth. I also model using an initial consonant to spell a word I don't know. When I get to the picture of my brother, I say, "Hmmm, that's my brother, but I don't know how to write 'brother'—so I'm just going to write the sounds I do know. What sounds does 'brother' start with? B-B-rother?" "B!" the students respond, and so I write "B" next to the picture of my brother.

Throughout our writing we continue to use this strategy for writing down words we don't know how to spell. Later we'll use the foundation of initial sounds to lay the groundwork for adding middle and ending sounds in our writing as well, as discussed in the section Invented Spelling on page 18.

Planning Out Words

As my students become more comfortable with writing workshop, they begin to see themselves as writers. Elijah asked one day, "How do you spell 'I went to the park with my mom and my grandma and I had fun.'" Elijah had previously been working on telling stories through his pictures only. He then moved to labeling his pictures. Now he had a sense that he could write down longer thoughts to accompany his pictures. Many other children asked for the same kind of help in writing full sentences.

Hindy List, a staff developer who works in my classroom, modeled a technique for our class that helps students like Elijah. She shows students how to plan out their words. She says the sentence aloud a few times with the child and then draws lines on the paper for where the words would go. For example, with Elijah, she simplified the sentence (with the intention of later helping the student add more words) to say: *I went to the park.* Then Hindy wrote _____ _____ _____ _____ _____, leaving a space for each word Elijah wanted to write and saying each word as she drew the line where it would go. She then went back to each space and had Elijah write down the sounds he heard. Elijah wrote: *I wt to the pk.* After writing initial sounds and using invented spelling, Elijah and Hindy reread the sentence they just wrote. Now Elijah was ready to work on the rest of his thoughts. Together Hindy and Elijah would plan out the words he wanted to write and then figure out the sounds together.

Hindy and I present this technique in a mini-lesson for the whole class and reinforce the strategy during writing conferences. Planning out the words helps children isolate words in a sentence. In this way they can more easily focus on the individual sounds for each word. In addition, separating the sentences into words gives the students a feeling of independence. Whereas writing an entire sentence may feel daunting, working on a few words or sounds at a time is much more manageable.

Using this technique helps students focus on the initial sounds of the words. Often a student comes up to me and says, "How do you spell 'house'?" And as soon as I start to sound it out for her, she says, "I already have the 'H.'" This is wonderful! Students are independently using initial sounds and now moving beyond those sounds in their writing. Both the labeling structures and planning out the words are tools that foster that independence.

Invented Spelling

I expect my students to use invented spelling. Although I expect them to know several frequently used words and provide a word wall as a resource, I encourage my students to free themselves of the need to spell everything accurately. In their zeal to spell correctly, they lose their ideas and the voice in their writing. In kindergarten and first grade I want to foster their creativity, and I encourage them to get their thoughts down in any way they can. Of course, I show them how to use classroom resources, such as book basket labels, charts we've made together, and our "kid of the day list," which has all of our classmates' names on it. We also study word families in conjunction with our poem of the week or to extend the study of a word we add to our word wall. However, I also show them how to stretch out a word, how to make a good guess, and how to listen to the sounds in the beginning, middle, and end of the word.

Diane Snowball, in her book, *Ideas for Spelling* (Heinemann, 1993), writes:

> Learning to write, like learning to talk, is a developmental process. When learning to talk, children are doing so for a purpose. Because their approximations are accepted and encouraged, they confidently explore the rules governing oral language. By allowing children to explore written language, we allow them to discover its purposes and feel confident about attempting to write words they may not know how to spell. Through this exploration, children acquire knowledge about the nature of the orthography (or written language) and naturally assume a greater responsibility for their own writing. Children who are allowed to experiment, and whose questions about words and spelling are answered, will begin to formulate and later refine ideas about spelling in the same way as they formulated and refined their spoken language.
>
> Children's invented spellings are the learners' attempts to find pattern and order in the spelling system. It is important that writers of all ages are afforded the same conditions for learning to spell as those offered to beginning writers. By being allowed to continue to take risks when attempting unknown words, writers will gradually move towards conventional spelling as they further explore the relationships between the oral and written language. Some invented spelling is more advanced than others (that is, they more closely resemble conventional spellings). By observing such approximations, insights may be gained into what the writer knows and doesn't know about spelling. This in turn provides guidelines for teaching. If children are not allowed opportunities to attempt spellings of unknown words, it is not possible to teach according to their needs.

I encourage my students to use invented spelling in their first drafts. It is only when we get to the publishing phase of our writing that I formally ask students to revisit words they should know, or direct them to the word wall as a resource (see page 25). During writing conferences I consistently encourage students to spell frequently used words conventionally. I also model using the word wall as a resource, as well as using word families and sounds to make a reasonable guess about how a word is spelled.

The trade-off is clear to me: the chance to get down a wonderful thought, albeit with a few misspelled words, or the missed opportunity to put that thought down in writing because the writer feels stifled or unable to come up with the conventional spelling. This freedom can mean the difference between a mediocre story and one that captures a child's true voice. For example, a child who wants to write, "I was so excited about going to the Six Flags I could barely fall asleep the night before," may instead write, "I went to Six Flags," because he only knows how to spell those words. The spelling can always be edited, but a child's true voice and passion are hard to recapture.

▲▲▲▲▲▲▲▲▲▲▲▲▲▲

Writing workshop in kindergarten and first grade is about inspiring and enabling children to tell stories that they are passionate about. It is also about capturing those children's stories and spirit on paper. Every child is a storyteller through pictures, sounds, labels, words, and sentences. I try to inspire my children to do the work of writers and share their stories.

Finding and Telling Our Stories

My goal for the year is to inspire my students to tell their stories through pictures and words. To do this, I plan a few units of study that will give them opportunities to tell their stories through different genres. It is my hope that the variety of genres, along with the mini-lessons and discussions about writers, craft, and inspiration, will give them the tools they need to tell their stories confidently.

Throughout the year we study several different genres of writing together. Our timeline looks roughly like this:

Timeline Overview

Early September	True and About You Stories
Late September/October	Writing Groups/ True and About You Stories
November	Pattern Books
December	True and About You Books
January/February	Poetry Study
March/April	Letter-writing
May/June	Student Choice

Although this book concentrates primarily on our poetry study, it may be helpful to know a little bit about the kinds of experiences my students have in preparation for the poetry work later in the year.

True and About You Stories

When I started student teaching in an EK/K classroom with Elena Davis, I wasn't sure what young children could write about or how to capture their amazing stories on paper. Elena modeled for me asking the students to write stories that were "true and about you" during writer's workshop. She recognized that children are experts about their own lives and that their lives are their most developmentally appropriate writing topic. In addition, writing about themselves gives them a specific pool of knowledge to pull from, whereas writing about imaginary friends or superheroes did not. Therefore, I, too, adopted the "true and about you" approach for encouraging young writers.

The focus of my "True and

Children love writing "true and about you" stories. The kindergartner's pictures (shown below at left) tell a true story about her relationship with her sister.

The first grader (work shown below at right) uses both labeling and planning out words to tell his story: "I was sick. I cried. It was night."

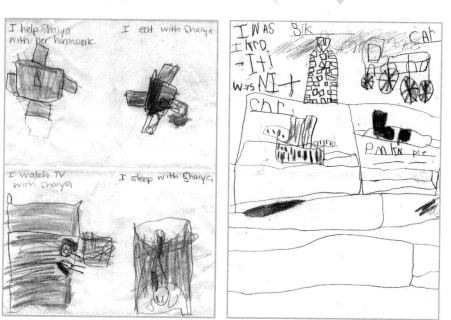

About You" unit is to give all of my students a way to feel successful in telling their own stories. Some students come in knowing how to write some words and sentences, whereas others are still working on learning their letters and sounds. This unit allows children to tell their stories in any way they can. For some, that means using only pictures or labels; for others, it means writing a multi-page story.

Most importantly, though, I want my students to feel comfortable taking risks with their writing. I want to give them structures and strategies they can add to their toolboxes to help them become competent writers. The components that follow serve as a structure for optimizing risk taking and student success.

Pattern Books

As students become more assured as writers, I want them to move beyond one-page stories. They can and do write more given an appropriate structure. Around early November, I move them into writing pattern books. From our reading workshop, my students are familiar with Sunshine Books and others that follow a pattern. For example, the book *Building With Blocks* reads: A red block, a green block, a yellow block, a blue block, a black block, a white block, a rocket ship. Often the patterns are even more similar as in the book *I Like:* I like _____, I like _____, I like _____, I like _____ and I like _____. Using these books as a model, I ask my class to write pattern books of their own. Together we create a chart of good pattern book starters. Each day as we begin our writing workshop we revisit our pattern book starters and add some more to the list. One year, we came up with these starters:

☀ I like…	☀ I can…	☀ I hear…
☀ I am…	☀ I see…	☀ I make…
☀ This is me…	☀ I feel…	☀ I read…
☀ I go…	☀ I eat…	
☀ I play…	☀ I dream…	

I post our chart in the room and also make a copy of our first day's starters for each child's writing folder. Having the pattern book starters in their folders makes it easier for them to use them as a resource.

The move towards pattern books takes our writing in a new direction. Primarily, it enables students to feel successful writing more than one page to create actual books. This is extremely rewarding for them. Secondly, it gives students a tool that helps them write more words more easily. Using the same line to start each page enables the children to sound out only one or two words at the end of the page. Many children find this a relief, as sounding out words is hard work. I also find that, by the end of the book they have written, students have indeed learned to write the pattern independently, without referring back to their sheet. This activity enhances their sight word knowledge and develops their independence as writers.

The children also enjoy writing books that are similar to the books they are reading. The connection between their take-home books and their writing is natural, as their sense of themselves as writers and readers begins to evolve. Also, it is easy for other students in the class to read the work of their classmates: once the pattern is established, the pictures support the rest of the text. This promotes interdependence in the classroom, and students begin to use one another as writing experts and resources.

A first-grader's pattern book, using the "I go" starter. ▶

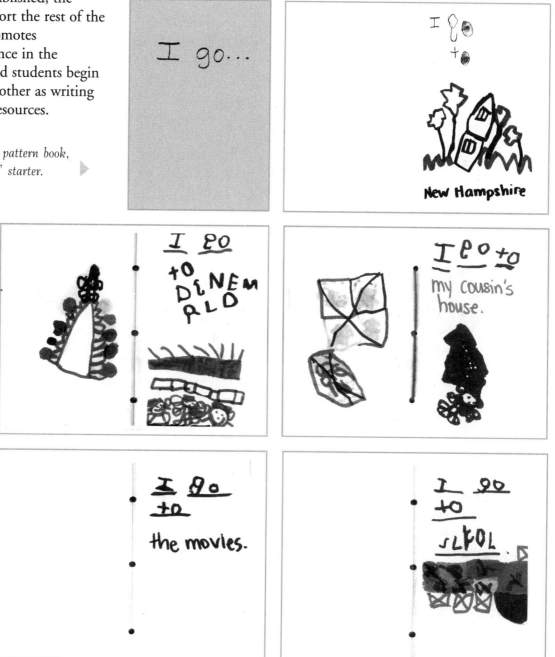

Moving Beyond Pattern Books

Writing pattern books gives students a great sense of accomplishment. The patterns are easy to think of and easy to write. After two weeks, however, many students are ready to move beyond the structure of the pattern book.

Around late November, then, we move from pattern books to personal narratives and book making. My mini-lessons concentrate on telling a longer family story, and I model working on the same story for several days. I model the structures and routines that I want students to continue using. Because I want them to build upon their existing writing skills, I continue modeling how to plan words and use pictures with details to support the words. I use the word wall (see page 25) to help me find a word I don't know. I show the students how I reread my story each day and add new details to it. We talk about adding pages to a book, if necessary. The children enjoy hearing the story on a daily basis, and they look forward to each new installment. This process transfers to their own writing as they begin to write longer stories with more details, using both words and pictures.

I also add new paper to the writing center: pre-made books and lined story-paper. Since many students ask me for help stapling books together during writing time, the pre-made books free me to concentrate on conferences rather than on stapling books. The lined story paper gives students room for pictures, and the lines remind them to leave room for words.

We play tennis.

I took a break.

This first grader used the "I play" pattern as a starting point and developed a true story.

My coach taught me to play tennis

I won a tennis trophy.

My Mom clapped.

The "So What?" of the Story

Some students have trouble moving beyond the "I went to the park. I had fun" stories. Whereas in the beginning of the year that start is wonderful, by late fall I want to push my students to see their stories as even more. I want them to have a reason for writing about a certain experience. In November, I begin to challenge them about their topics. As a class we discuss the reason for telling stories, and in the gentlest, kindest, most caring way, I ask my students, "What's the so what of your story? So what about the park? What did you do there? Who were you with? Why is it important to tell this story?"

My students respond to this. They understand that my "so what" is not mean or teasing; rather, it is a probe to get them to think more deeply about their writing. I model for them using this with each other. I encourage them to ask each other, "So what? So what about your story is so important?" They guide one another to write and use specific ideas to enhance their stories.

Personal and Classroom Word Walls

The word wall is an effective resource for my beginning writers. It starts as a blank bulletin board marked only with the upper and lower case letters of the alphabet. Throughout the year, during our mini-lessons, we add frequently used words to the word wall. Often we add words from our weekly poems. Together we discuss why we choose a word for the word wall and where it should go. This gives us an opportunity to explore the initial sounds in the word and locate the letter under which it should be placed on the wall. As our wall grows, adding new words gives us a chance to review the words already there and an opportunity to compare similar words such as *the, them, they, there,* and *then.* We share strategies for deciding which word is which.

During the year the way we use the word wall changes. In the beginning of the year it is there for reference, although many students are not yet comfortable using it as such. They understand where to place words and how to find them, but they fail to use it as a consistent tool. As the year progresses I continue to direct the students back to the word wall for commonly used

Our classroom word wall—we continue to add words to it throughout the year.

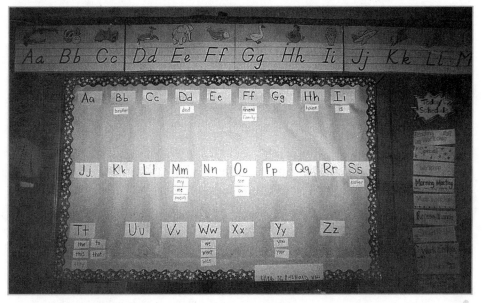

words. When they ask me how to spell a word, we'll go to the wall and locate the word. I encourage the students to bring their writing to the wall and copy the word directly onto their papers. Other teachers have Velcro word walls so that students can take words back to their seats. No matter how it looks or works, the wall needs to be accessible for students—it should be at their eye level and on a manageable scale.

About three months into the school year, I give students their own copies of our word wall. I leave room for them to add their own words. During writing conferences I add words to their lists that they may need. For example, if Rennick is writing a book about a trip to Jamaica, I add the word "Jamaica" to his word list, since this is a word he will use frequently throughout his writing piece. Throughout the year I reissue updated copies of our classroom word wall.

_____s Word List

Aa	Bb	Cc	Dd	Ee	Ff	Gg
all	boys	come	do		friend	girl
and	by	can	dog			go
are	back	came	day			got
at	ball					get
						good

Hh	Ii	Jj	Kk	Ll	Mm	Nn
have	in		Kid	little	my	no
how	it			like	me	not
had	is				myself	
house	I'm				mom	
	I'd					

Oo	Pp	Qq	Rr	Ss	Tt
on				said	the
our				small	they
of				silly	then
				seed	them
				see	to
					this

Uu	Vv	Ww	Xx	Yy	Zz
up		where		yes	
		when			
		went			
		was			
		were			
		will			

▲▲▲▲▲▲▲▲▲▲▲▲▲▲

From pattern books to word walls, I have filled my classroom with supports for writing. Over the first few months we spend time practicing our writing routines, discussing where to look for words, and discovering how patterns can help us with our writing. Now that my students are comfortable in their routines, and their words and images are beginning to spill out of their folders, we're ready for another challenge— writing poetry.

Introducing Poetry

From the very first day of school, poetry begins our day, filters through our day, and ends our day. Even before beginning a formal poetry study, the children are informally introduced to poetry in a variety of ways. I choose a poem for shared reading every week. I lead recitations of poems during transitions between activities (i.e., by the time we finish saying this poem together everyone should be in line or on the rug). Students gather poems into anthologies. I use poems for movement activities, math lessons, science lessons, and reading centers. Children unconsciously develop the concept of what defines a poem and how poems differ from stories and books. It's not until children have an enormous amount of informal experience with poetry that I begin a poetry study with them.

Once we begin, we do so very slowly. We work first as a whole class, deciding and defining what exactly a poem is and what it looks like. We then work in small groups to write poems. We move from groups to poetry partners and finally to writing poetry independently. This carefully constructed timeline gives our class the time to linger on defining and redefining poetry for ourselves.

Overview of Poetry Unit

Day 1–3
- ☼ Poetry Game (whole class)
  Introduce terms for list and circle poems
- ☼ Group Poems
  (Introduce poetry paper)

Day 4–5
- ☼ Poetry Game (child recorder)
- ☼ Partner Poems

Day 6–8
- ☼ Independent Poems
- ☼ List Poems/ Poetry Walks
- ☼ I see; I hear; I smell; I notice; I feel…

Day 9/ Weeks 2–4
- ☼ Independent Poems
- ☼ Exploring Poem Structures Through Mini-Lessons (see next chapter)

Shared Reading

In her book, *On Solid Ground* (Heinemann, 2000), Sharon Taberski writes, "During Shared Reading, the teacher reads a Big Book or enlarged text with the children, who are sitting up close so they can see it and read along. The texts are ones the children may not be able to read independently, but can read successfully in unison with the teacher and their classmates."
I find poems perfect for shared reading.

Poem of the Week

My students' first exposure to poetry comes on the first day of school, when I introduce the first poem of the poems I choose each week for shared reading.

The poem may relate to a class theme, a word study, or a writing idea. I also tend to choose short poems, no longer than about 12 lines. I choose poems that promise to be easily digestible during our week-long study. Each week I look through the books on the poetry shelf in my classroom and choose a poem related to a classroom theme, to the season, the weather, a class trip, or special school event. I look for poems that have descriptive language, but descriptions to which young students can relate. Sometimes I choose rhyming poems, but not always. The rhymes are generally good because they are predictable and easy for emergent readers to decode. On the other hand, I try not to always select a rhyming poem because I want my students to understand that poetry is more than just rhymes. Throughout the year, I try to choose poems with varied subjects so I can share with my students the breadth of topics poetry can cover.

After choosing a poem, I rewrite it on large chart paper for all to see and use during shared reading. Each day during the week, I use the poem for various purposes, which I outline below.

Monday

We read the poem three times together. The repetition allows children to chime in by the end of the third reading. Children can also listen for rhythm, rhyme, and phrasing. Rhyme is a particularly important feature because it helps beginning readers predict the text. Later in the year children often can read the entire poem without listening to it first.

Tuesday

We read the poem together once and then begin to find "word wall words," or words we know. One student at a time comes up to the poem and underlines a familiar word. I say, "Who can find *you?*" And a student comes up and underlines the word with a colored marker. "Who can find *no?*" And another student comes up to underline the text. "Is there another place where it says *no?*" We continue to find and underline frequently used words. Then we reread the poem chorally: I read the non-underlined text and students read the underlined familiar words. Beyond memorization, this activity focuses the students on the text. It helps them to recognize and pull out the words they already are familiar with. By underlining and then reading aloud our word wall words, children feel less intimidated by the poem—they now know that there are many words in the poem that they can read. This gives them the confidence they need to tackle words they don't immediately recognize.

Wednesday

We read the poem once together before finding more familiar words— perhaps more word wall words, or other words that are common but not yet on our word wall. We also look for words that we may want to add to our word wall. For example, when we were studying water in our class science study, we decided that *water* and *rain* were two words that we wanted to add to our word wall, since we would be using them frequently in our discussions and in our writing, and they were found in many poems we read relating to that theme. Once again, children come up and underline familiar words and some challenge words. I continue my questioning: "Who can find the word *water?* What would it start with? What would it end with? What other sounds do you hear in the middle?" This shared activity stretches their thinking and enables the entire class to participate in finding the word and thinking about the sounds of the word. After finding these

Potato
Grandfather said:
"Here's some news for you lasses.
Potatoes have eyes
But they don't wear glasses.
They don't go to sleep,
They shed no tears,
They have no chins,
They have no ears,
Their skins are brown,
They have no curls.
Now remember this, boys and girls."
Silly grandfather!

This poem shows the word work we did that week.

words we once again reread the poem in choral mode: I read the non-underlined text and students read the words they now know. The choral reading gives the students an active role in the process, focusing them on the words we just identified and allowing them to hear the words pronounced by others.

Thursday

After reading the poem, we look for rhymes, patterns, or more challenge words—words that may be specific to the poem, but not in our common realm of knowledge, such as *potato* and *glasses*. These patterns and rhymes help us to predict the text. Children come up and circle the rhyming words. In addition we use this time to talk about reading strategies and making guesses about a text based on its rhyming pattern.

Jodi: [reading poem aloud] *Dream of a weed, growing from a seed, quietly, quietly from a _____.* (I point to the next word) What could that word be?

Julia: Seed.

Jodi: How did you know?

Julia: It rhymes with weed.

Jodi: Anyone else? Who had another strategy for figuring out that word?

Eli: It starts with an "S" and rhymes with weed.

Logan: I know that "s-e-e-d" is seed.

When we read a poem that does not rhyme, we talk about the structure of the poem, the beautiful language, the meaning of the poem, or the images that the language of the poem provides. For humorous poems we discuss what makes them funny, and children share their understanding of the poem. They are becoming fluent at reading the poem. By this point in the week they are eager to show their knowledge and once again we read the poem in choral mode. Usually there are only a few non-underlined words left for me to read and they fill in the blanks with the rest.

Friday

We read the poem once together and then the children read it aloud as a class to me. It's amazing how they have learned so much in so few days. Also on Friday, I rewrite the poem on a "poem card" (a large piece of poster board) and add it to the classroom poetry collection. The next week we start all over again with a new poem.

Using poetry as shared reading gives our class an inviting introduction to reading a new text. After exploring a poem for the week, it becomes part of our class, recited during transitions between lessons, or as we line up, or discussed in comparison with another poem or book.

Poetry Anthologies

At the end of each week, children also add a copy of the poem, which they have illustrated, to their own poetry anthologies. By the end of the year, children have a beautifully illustrated collection of special poems that they can read.

Using a report cover and clear top-loading sheet protectors, I create a poetry anthology for each student. I anticipate that we will cover 40 poems together over the course of the year. Keeping that in mind, I fill each report cover with 20 sheet protectors. (Each one holds two poems back to back.) At the end of each week I provide students with a typed copy of the poem we explored that week. I also provide them with a special set of art materials to illustrate their poems. The poet, the subject of the poem, and the variety of materials previously used inspire the choice of art materials. I want to give the students a plethora of materials and styles to explore during the year. For example, for a Shel Silverstein poem, I had the children use only black felt tip pens. I showed them Shel Silverstein's illustrations and invited them create illustrations inspired by his art.

Jodi: Today we are going to illustrate "Lazy Jane." Shel Silverstein writes and illustrates his poems. [I hold up *Where the Sidewalk Ends* and show it to the class.] Let's look at Shel Silverstein's illustrations. What do you notice about his art?

Liana: He doesn't use colors.

Eddie: He only uses black.

Asatta: He just draws the outside part.

Jodi: When you illustrate your poems today, you may want to try to illustrate your poems just like Shel Silverstein. On your tables you'll find thin black pens to help you with your illustrations.

For a poem about the rain with the line, "with silver liquid drops" we used cotton swabs and silver paint to make silver drops on our poems. Although everyone uses the same materials, each illustration is unique.

Other ideas for art materials include:

- markers only (no black or brown)
- colored pencils
- crayons
- watercolors
- tissue paper
- tissue paper and black felt pen for details
- watercolors and black felt pen for details
- creating borders that relate to the poem
- tempera paints
- rubber stamps
- limiting the colors used, i.e., only blues, or only blues and greens (for water)
- mimicking the style of an artist (tissue paper for Eric Carle)
- ripped or cut paper collage
- crayon and watercolor combinations
- rubbings
- oil pastels
- charcoal

After the children illustrate their poems, I collect them and then assemble them into their anthologies. As they grow, the anthologies become part of our classroom library. They are easily accessible for students to read alone or with a partner during reading workshop.

Seed Pods
by Terry Cooper

Maple tree twigs
flounce a jig
in the big
wind,

Shooting
plumed pods
high
into butterfly sky.

Wrinkled and dry,
spinning,
they fly
into gutters,
gardens, and
grass.
By and by,
some grow,
some die.

Dream of a Weed
by Margaret Wise Brown

Dream of a weed growing from a seed
Quietly, quietly from a seed
In a garden
A slim green weed
Quietly, quietly from a seed.

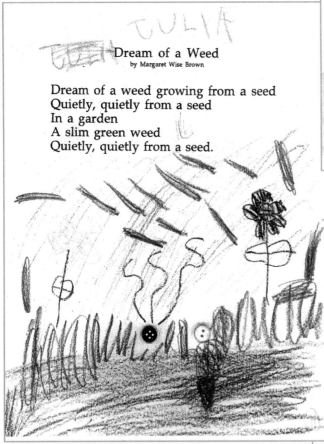

Potato
by Mary Steele

Grandfather said:
"Here's some news for you lasses.
Potatoes have eyes
But they don't wear glasses.
They don't go to sleep,
They shed no tears,
They have no chins,
They have no ears.
Their skins are brown,
They have no curls.
Now remember this, boys and girls."
....Silly Grandfather

▲ *Illustrated poems for poetry anthologies. Students used water color and crayons for "Seed Pods," buttons and crayons for "Dream of a Weed," and collage, googly eyes, and marker for "Potato."*

Reading Poetry Aloud

Beyond our shared reading of poetry, I want the children to hear many poems read aloud. Each day during our unit of study, I read aloud three to five poems.

I often start our morning meeting with a poem. I point out the "Poetry Shelf," which holds all of our poetry books (see page 30 for a list of Favorite Poetry Books). Each day I pick a poetry book off the shelf and read from it. Many times the children want more than just the few I select. Some poems are humorous, others are about school issues, friends, dreams, and so on. I try to find poems that my students can connect to in some way. We read poems about food and lunchtime. We read poems about people. We read poems about things we notice. Each poem we read gives students more experience with the sound of poetry. In addition, reading the poems aloud gives us more opportunities to talk about the poems, their meanings, and the language the poet used. In contrast to shared reading, where the focus is on the words in the text in addition to the meaning, the focus of the read aloud is the sound of the poem and its beautiful language.

▲▲▲▲▲▲▲▲▲▲▲▲▲▲

Poems are favorite friends in our classroom now. We use them for read alouds, when we line up, while we're waiting to start our morning meeting and a few stragglers are still at their cubbies. We've got the sound, rhythm, and images of poetry in our heads, and now we are ready to try writing some of our own.

Some Guiding Questions for Poetry

- What does this poem remind you of?
- Close your eyes and listen. What kinds of pictures do you see as I read this poem?
- What do you think the poet meant when he or she wrote: _____?
- Why do you think the poet chose to use that word?
- Stand up; let's act this poem out together.

Beginning Poetry Writing

have high expectations for my students as poets. I want them to write more words and capture their poetic sayings on paper. I also want them to make connections between the poems we read and their own subjects for poetry. However, I am always nervous that these expectations are too high. In order to ensure success, I know that I must teach poetry *very slowly* and take my cues from the kids on how to proceed.

The Paper Bag Game

When I begin our unit on poetry, I don't tell children immediately what we will be studying. Instead I invented the Paper Bag Game to introduce it. I originally learned this game to teach children about using their senses to help them be keen observers as scientists. I now use the same game to record the colorful language in my classroom.

I put five classroom objects in a brown paper lunch bag (marker, ball, paintbrush, Lego, and paper clip). I then ask one student to stick a hand in the bag and, without telling the other students what it is, describe it to them. The rest of the class has to guess what the object is based on its description. The describer can tell the class how the object feels or what it is used for. As the child describes the object, I record the descriptions in list form on a piece of chart paper. Once the class guesses the object, I use the name of the object as the title of the list, which is now our poem.

Here's one example:

Marker

Smooth
Clip
Fat and round
Two pieces
For drawing
Smelly
Marker

The first day we play this game, the children describe and I transcribe. We talk about carefully choosing words to describe the objects and making a list about the object as we do so. After creating the list, I read it in my poet voice (see next page), and ask the children what the list sounds like. "A poem!" they shout, and our poetry unit is off and running.

The following day we play the Paper Bag Game again, this time with different objects. I ask a child to transcribe the descriptions this time. Each time a description is given, the class helps our transcriber figure out what letters to write. In this way, the student transcriber models what the children will be doing the next day. I want children to feel free to use invented spelling, and also to notice how the poem goes down the page, rather than across—more like a list than a story. At right is a poem (translated from the invented spelling) that the students wrote on the second day of a poetry unit.

Writing Pen

Smooth
Metal
Fat and thin
Round
For writing
Black
Writing Pen

Several students model transcribing while others model describing the objects in the bag that day. We name these "List Poems" and "Circle Poems" and begin a class chart about the kinds of poems we know how to write. "List Poems" they define as poems that are lists. "Circle Poems" are poems that start and end the same way. We add these concepts to our developing poetry knowledge.

Using a "Poet Voice"

As I read these newly created poems to the class I use my "poet voice." I read softly and smoothly and take the time to make a pause with my voice after each line break. I use this poet voice, this deliberate slow and soft tone, whenever I read newly written poems in our class. I model using that voice so the children can hear the "sound of the poems." As I do this, the children often say, "YOU made it sound like a poem." I tell them I do. We talk about how to do that and I ask them to read the poems with me using their poet voices. This conversation about reading poetry aloud gives children insight on how to read their own poetry and how to write it. As they read aloud and pause their voices with the line breaks, they begin to think about the line breaks in their own poems and how they will sound when read aloud. During the rest of the unit we encourage each other to use those "poet voices" when sharing our work.

Writing Poetry in Small Groups

When I feel that students understand how to play the Paper Bag Game, we are ready for the next step. The next day we begin with one whole-class Paper Bag Game description and then children gather in their writing groups to work. Each writing group writes about a different object. I use ordinary classroom objects such as a starfish, the fish tank, the class gerbils, fresh flowers, a pet cricket, Legos—anything that they can observe. I specifically choose to give them objects that they can touch or look at up close so that they can carefully observe them before they write. I set out the objects before the lesson so they are ready for students to use at their tables. Only during this introductory phase do I choose the subject matter of the poems. At this point, I want students to focus on the form and not get bogged down in choosing a subject.

I ask each group to produce one poem together. Therefore, one child, or a few children, write, and some illustrate the poem. This kind of cooperative learning is difficult for young children, so I model working together before sending them off.

Jodi: Today you are going to work in your writing groups to create a poem together about an object. On your tables you will find a special object. You will all need to help one another observe it carefully and think of what ideas to add to your list poem. Here is the special paper you will use for your poetry. [Show poetry paper.] What do you think this box is for? [Point to box at top.]

Will: That's for the pictures.

Jodi: Right. And what do you think these lines are for?

Vinny: That's where the words go.

Jodi: Remember that when you write poetry the words will go down that page. This paper will help you write that way. One person from each group will do the writing. Everyone else in the group will have to help that person figure out the sounds to write, just as we did when we played the "Paper Bag Game" as a class. Remember how you all helped me write the words? It is your job to each give ideas for the poem and help your friends write the words. Who thinks they understand and can share it with the class?

Isa: We're all going to write poems in groups. One person is going to do the writing and the other people are going to help them with the ideas and sounds.

Jodi: Super. Let's get started.

Name:

Date:

One of my groups wrote about the crickets and cricket cage in our classroom, another about the fresh flowers on the table, another about a starfish we had on a shelf, and the last about a large seashell. The cricket group wrote:

Crickets

Crickets
They live in cardboard
Make a sound with
6 legs
Walk
Eats rotten apples
Small pool

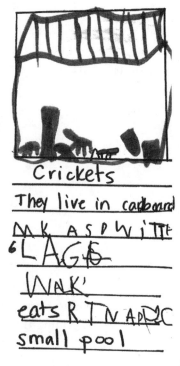

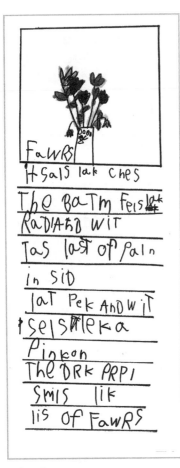

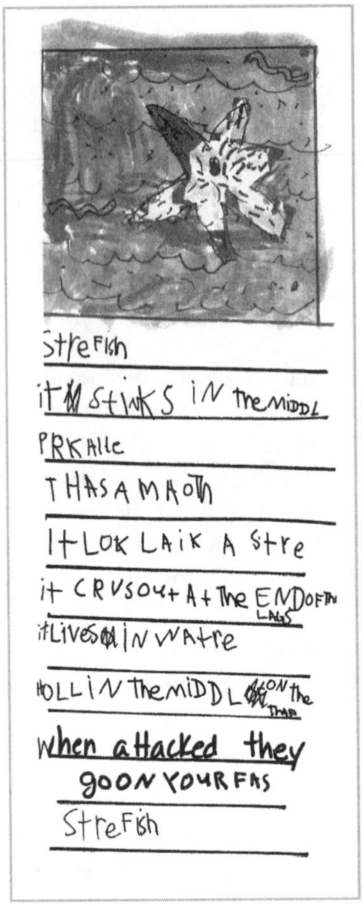

The handwritten child writing (flower group):

FaWRS
It Sals lak ches
The BaTm Feisl
RaDIaD wiT
Tas last off Paln
in SiD
laT Pek AnD wiT
i Sel Shl ek a
Pink on
The DRk PRPl
Smils lik
liS of FaWRS

The handwritten child writing (starfish group):

StreFsh
it StinkS iN the miDDl
PRKAlle
THASAMAoth
It LoK LAiK a Stre
it CRVSOut A+ the ENDOFm LAgS
itLivesoq iN wAtre
HoLL iN the miDDL ON the THAP
when attacked they
goon Your FAs
StreFish

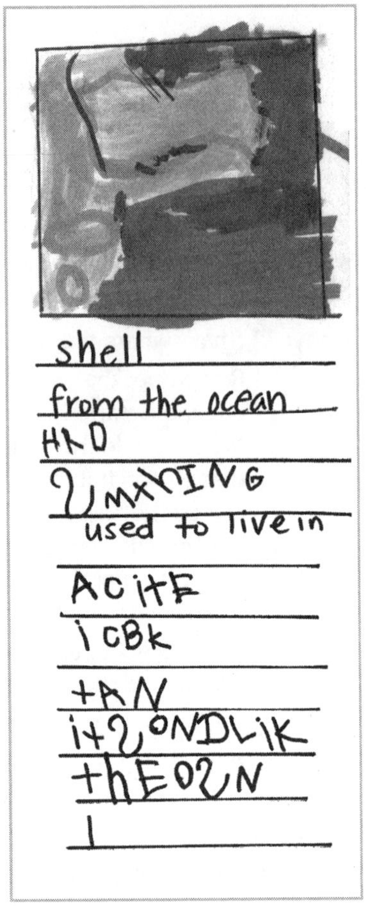

The handwritten child writing (shell group):

shell
from the ocean
HRD
SumxTING
used to live in
AC iTE
i CBk
+AN
it SoNDLik
thE O2N
I

The flower group wrote:

Flowers

Flowers
It smells like cheese
The bottom feels like sticky
Red and white
There's lots of pollen
inside
Lot of pink and white
Smells like a
pine cone
The dark purple
smells like
lots of flowers

The starfish group wrote:

Starfish

Starfish
It stinks in the middle
Prickly
It has a mouth
It curves out at the end of the legs
It lives in watery
Hole in the middle on the top
When attacked they
Go on your face
Starfish

The shell group wrote:

Shell

Shell
From the Ocean
Hard
Something
Used to live in
it
It can break
Tan
It sounds like
The ocean

After writing in groups, we get together and share and celebrate these amazing poems. I am always excited to see that students really seem to be describing the objects and taking risks with this new form of writing. In this particular class, I felt that giving the students one more day of group work would give those who were less confident about their writing another day to see how the process worked.

The following day we again broke up into our writing groups. I gave each group a new object. To three of the groups I gave a roll of "Smarties" candy, and to the other group I gave a roll of five different ribbons: one silver, one yellow, one pink, one green, and one purple. The task was the same as the day before, to describe the object in list form. Some children wrote, and others illustrated, but everyone contributed to the group's poem.

The candy groups wrote these:

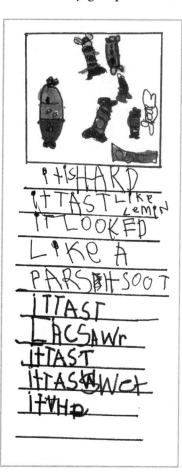

Candy

It is hard
It tastes like lemon
It looked
Like a
Parachute
It tastes
Like strawberry
It tastes
It tastes wet
It's very good

Candy

It's
Hard candy
It's
Soft
It is color-
ful
They crack open
When you
Tap them a lot
It's good
It is wet

Candy

It tastes good
It has a lot of colors

The ribbon group wrote:

> **Ribbons**
> Colorful
> Ribbon
> Rainbow

Once again, at the end of the writing period, I was impressed. We shared the poems and the pictures and looked closely at the object described. Everyone agreed that the groups had done a good job describing their objects. I reminded the children that these were called "list poems"—the kind of poem that looks like a list that not only catalogues a subject's characteristics but also captures its essential spirit.

Writing Poetry with Partners

Although I felt that the unit was going smoothly with this group, I wanted to ensure that all children would be successful. I knew that I still had some children who weren't writing many letters or words independently and that they would be overwhelmed by the task of writing a poem by themselves. Therefore, after the group writing experience, I divided the class into writing partners. In selecting partners, I pair stronger writers with struggling writers. In this way I give those who are struggling with writing a way to record their voice.

We had recently visited the Staten Island Children's Zoo, and we had just released our butterflies from our butterfly garden—both fascinating experiences for my children. After releasing the butterflies, Asatta and I had a conversation.

Asatta: Will we see them again?
Jodi: No.
Asatta: I will miss those butterflies.
I wish I could keep those butterflies.
I'm going to visit those butterflies.
They are so pretty.

During our writing mini-lesson that morning, I shared that conversation with the class and wrote down Asatta's words on some poetry paper.

I told them that Asatta's words sounded to me like a poem, and they agreed. We talked about other shared experiences that we could write about with our partners. Many children talked about the butterflies and the trip to the zoo, and off they went with their writing partners to write about a shared experience. We also talked about how, when writing a poem, you don't need to tell the whole story—you can just tell little parts of it. Vinny and Keiji produced the poem at right (Keiji wrote, Vinny drew).

We write with poetry partners for two days. By the end of the second day, many children are eager to start their own poems. I am usually satisfied by then that the children understand their task and are trying their hand with invented spelling. The following day we continue our poetry work independently.

Butterflies

Butterflies
are very
nice
They are
zig zag
and polka-dot
They
fly
a lot
Butterflies

Writing Poetry Independently

Over the next few days I model writing poetry during my writer's workshop mini-lessons. I always use the poetry paper and model drawing a picture and telling a story through short phrases.

The content of my mini-lessons varies, from working on making the words go down the page, to using short phrases, to just generating ideas for what to write about. My focus is getting children to write letters and words. I want them to feel confident that they can express their beautiful language through the written word as well as through oral language. I initially choose not to focus on the white space of a poem, or line breaks, or even on many different kinds of poems. I merely want this to be an introduction that they later revisit and build upon. Later in our unit we may explore these topics a bit, depending on student interest and needs. In subsequent grades they will write poetry and think about line breaks, white space, and kinds of poems, but in kindergarten and first grade I want them to discover the power of words to express feelings. And, more importantly, I want them to feel successful in doing so.

▲▲▲▲▲▲▲▲▲▲▲▲▲▲

As students begin working on their own poems, I still fear that the task will be overwhelming. I've asked them to capture their thoughts in words and phrases, and to do so in a way different from any they've tried before. To help them with this challenge, I model a type of poem that will be easy for them to imitate, a list poem, which I discuss in the next chapter.

Experimenting with Poetry

By this time, students are beginning to understand how to pick ideas for their poems and that poems can be about almost anything, big or small. The difficulty, then, is how to organize that information so that it looks and sounds like a poem. Making lists of descriptions about objects is a start; then children use the list form as a springboard to other kinds of poetry.

List Poems

Early in the poetry unit, the easiest type of poem to generate is a list poem, in which children literally make lists of what they observe. These observations are about objects, either ones in our classroom or observed on our poetry walks, or about the students themselves. The first week or more of writing poems independently, therefore, starts with me modeling different types of list poems. The following sections describe those mini-lessons and how they have inspired poets in my classroom.

"I See" Poems

I begin each mini-lesson with writing of my own. I tell the students a story and model writing it for them—either in poem, story, or book form, depending on the genre we are studying. On this day I wanted to introduce combining list poems with using "I see…" as a prompt.

Jodi: I take the subway to school and then I walk from the subway station. How many of you take the subway? How many of you walk to school? How about the bus? Well, whenever I walk to school I notice all of the things around me. I notice people, the newspapers they read, grownups walking with kids, stores, and I always notice the flower stands on the corner by the school. What kinds of things do you see when you walk to school?

Cristina: I see dogs.

Agim: I see kids.

Nicky: I see cars.

Gabrielle: I see subway cars.

Ashley: I see bicycles.

Jodi: Wow, that's starting to sound like a poem to me—you've inspired me. Today, I'm going to write a poem about all of the things I see on the way to school.

I begin to write in front of them. I write this poem and say the words aloud as I do. I ask the students to help me sound out some of the words. Together we produce this poem (my thoughts, their sounds and spellings):

> On my way to school
> I see
> stores
> people
> nwspaprs
> gronups with kids
> flowrs
> lots of flowrs
> flowrs on evrey
> krner.

Jodi: When you go off to write today, you might want to try making a list of things that you see on your way to school.

When the children went off to write on their own, some wrote poems in a similar style. Greta and Vinny wrote their own variations.

Greta wrote:

Riding in a Taxi
I see
People with
Pets
The sidewalk
And then
We are
At
P.S. 3

Vinny wrote:

On the airplane
I see
Clouds
I see water
I see land
I was high in
The sky.

Vinny was just beginning to know his sounds; therefore we worked together on many of the words. Often Vinny had great ideas, but felt intimidated because he couldn't get his ideas down on paper. I helped Vinny with the beginning and ending of his poem because I didn't want him to lose the beautiful poem he had just begun. Vinny dictated his ideas to me and I wrote the beginning of the poem for him, "On the airplane, I see…" Together we worked on the sounds for *clouds* and Vinny wrote *Ks*. We alternated writing words. Composing this poem gave Vinny a chance to be successful at expressing himself even though he was just beginning to figure out how to use his knowledge to do so independently.

The next day during writing workshop I continue to build upon the "I See" theme. I read the poem "Riding on the Train" by Eloise Greenfield to the class. I remind students of the work from the day before and use this poet's work to further inspire them.

Inspired by Eloise Greenfield's poem Isa wrote:

I see

I see flowers
I see houses
I see ants
I see buses
I see taxis
I see Thomas'
House.

"Riding on the Train"
By Eloise Greenfield

I see
Fences and fields
Barns and bridges
Stations and stores
Trees
Other trains
Horses and hills
Water tanks
Towers
Streams
Old cars
Old men
Roofs
Raindrops crawling backwards on the window.

Encouraged by the writing from the previous day, I continue to model ideas for poetry during my mini-lessons. One day I wrote more about the flowers that I see every day when I am coming to school and how happy they make me. Another day, I wrote about a walk I took on a beautiful sunny day. During both lessons the children listened to my story, watched me draw the pictures, and then helped me spell my words. During these mini-lessons they act as teachers, guiding me through my writing. When they go to work independently, they do the same, guiding their peers in their groups.

Flowers

On the way
To school
Pink
Red
Yellow
Orange
Purple
Makes me
Happy
Even in
The
Rain.

Sunshine Walk

I walked
And walked
In the sun
All day.
I walked
And walked
All over
The city.
I loved my
Walk.
I love my
City.

Although neither of these poems is going to win awards, I want to model for the children how they can write poetry about the same things that they write stories about. I want children to begin to draw on their experience and see any experience as an opportunity for a poem. They become detectives, finding places, moments, and objects that can serve as inspiration for poems. In this class, before beginning our writing the next day, we generated this chart, inspired by Georgia Heard's book on poetry, *Awakening the Heart*.

Places where poetry hides...

...in a garden ...in the attic ...in the garbage
...in outer space ...in your lunch box ...in your food
...in your lights ...in the sea ...under the rug
...shells ...in a book ...in the clouds
...stars ...in the sun ...in your book bags
...in the waves ....in pipes ...under the sand
...treasure boxes ...music ...in clocks ...in the city
...under shelves ...in classrooms ...in pockets
...houses ...in instruments ...under water
...in your imagination ...behind curtains
...cubbies ...animals/insects ...dust
...on the moon ...under pillows
...in the grass ...in your blanket
...in a box ...in your head

Moving Beyond "I See" with Poetry Walks

After working on "I See" poems for a few days, I gather children on the rug for our poetry mini-lesson and hand out clipboards with poetry paper already attached. (If you don't have clipboards, cardboard and rubber bands work well, too.) I remind them of the poems we have written previously about all of the things we see on the way to school, and announce that today we will be taking a poetry walk. To prepare them, I give them the "poetry walk talk," which goes something like this:

Jodi: Today we are going to go outside on a poetry walk. I'm going to ask you not to talk while we are on this short walk. You will need all of your senses to be the best poetry detectives you can be. You may want to write a poem about things you see, you hear, you smell, you feel—whatever it is that moves you. Notice things carefully, be observers of the littlest things and pull them into your poetry. As we walk we will stop sometimes to let you record your thoughts. If you don't know how to spell a word you can put down the first sound or draw a picture or ask a friend. The most important thing is that you get your thoughts down. When we come back to the classroom you'll have a few more minutes to capture your thoughts on paper before some poets share their work. Ready to be poem detectives?

Eagerly my students line up, armed with pencils and clipboards, to take on the city block around the school. We usually get no more than five feet past the school door before children begin feverishly writing. I stop to let them write and then we move on.

We move slowly around the two blocks that our walk covers. We go into a small hidden garden and find treasures of inspiration in ants and architecture. The children are always reluctant to end our walk and continue to write as we go back to our classroom.

Students jot down ideas during a poetry walk and then work with them in class.

The poetry walk is successful for a couple of reasons. It gives students easily accessible ideas about what to include in their poem—they merely have to look around and list their observations. And, since students can record their observations with words or pictures, it makes writing poetry accessible to even the most emergent writers. Declan recorded his thoughts with pictures and I later helped him record his words.

Donna used both pictures and words with her writing. She used pictures to help her continue writing when she didn't know how to spell the words.

"I see" poems using pictures and words.

The poetry walk also gives students a new appreciation for looking closely at objects and a model for capturing their careful observations in the form of a poem. In addition, students are introduced to using nature and one's environment as inspiration. For days afterward children beg to go on poetry walks. We go on a few more, each time refocusing our thoughts on *I see*, or *I hear*, or *I smell....* Every time we go the children find remarkable ways of recording their observations. These observations, an extension of our poetry game and list poems, begin taking on the form of some wonderful poetry. During one of our walks Marshall wrote:

I see a bench.
I see a book.
I see a bird.
I see a path.
I see a gate.
I see a T.V.
I see a black ball.
I see a garbage can.
I see a bench.
I see a camera.
I see a statue.
I see a chain.
I see a pipe.
I see a berry.
I see a piano.
I see a hole.

As our observations become more detailed, so does our poetry. Our list poems grow to be more than lists; they blossom into keen collections of observations. The students begin to incorporate their own knowledge and feelings into these poems, and this takes them to new heights in their poetry development. Liana wrote:

Ladybugs. Seagulls.
Green leaves. Tiny
Pieces of glass.
Needles. Rectangles.
Bricks. Flowers.
Fingernails. One grain
Of sand. Shoelaces.
Numbers. Polka-dots.

Lucian wrote and dictated:

Worms
Live
Under dirt
Sometimes
They go scribble
Scrabble when
They move.

Listening Poems

As we continue our poetry walks, students become more adept at using all their senses to observe their surroundings. Incorporating their knowledge of pattern starters from their work on pattern books, and using the form of their "I see" poems, students begin trying different constructions for recording their thoughts during the poetry walks.

Bryan used both "I hear" and "I see" in this poem:

I hear
Cars. I hear birds.
I hear chicks
I see flowers
I see doors
I see roofs
I see flowers
Dying
I see grass
I see flowers that
Are not dying
I see homes.

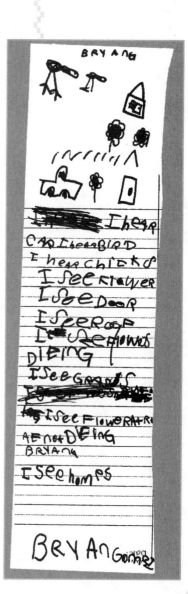

Bryan's confidence as a poet is evident as he flip-flops between the two patterns. As Bryan and others began to use these starters, I used their work as the focus of a mini-lesson.

Jodi:	Bryan tried something different when we went on a poetry walk yesterday. Bryan can you share with us the poem you wrote yesterday during our poetry walk?
Bryan:	[reads above poem]
Jodi:	What do you notice about the kind of list that Bryan made?
Ashley:	He wrote about things he saw.
Logan:	He wrote about things he heard.
Jodi:	Bryan used two patterns in his poem: "I see" and "I hear." That was a neat way to write his recordings. I'm wondering what other pattern starters we can think of that might be good starts for our poetry walks.
Liana:	I find…
Julia:	I smell…
Isa:	I feel…
Jodi:	These are starting to remind me of the patterns we used for our pattern books.
Students:	Yeah, me too!
Jodi:	When we go on our poetry walk today, you might want to try using a different start to express your observation. Maybe Bryan inspired you and you'd like to try to write a poem with "I hear" and "I see." Let's all remember to use our ears and our eyes, to listen as well as to look. What are some other ideas for poem starters you could try?

As the children share their ideas, I write down the list poem starters on chart paper. These starters are similar to the ideas we used when we wrote our pattern books earlier in the year. However, children are now using them in their poetry as well as their books. As students feel more confident with their poetry, they begin to internalize these structures and use them freely in their writing.

"I Find"

Liana used "I find…" as a start during one of our poetry walks. She wrote:

> I find a heart.
> I find a picture.
> I find a tree. I find
> A building. I find
> A bush. I find
> Flowers. I find a
> School. I find moss.
> I find grass.
> I find bumblebees.
> I find fish.
> I find gerbils.
> I find books.
> I find a rug.
> I find a bookshelf.

After our poetry walk that day, I asked Liana to share her poem. I chose her because I wanted the class to see how, inspired by Bryan's idea, Liana used a new starter for her work. I want to encourage students to borrow ideas from their peers. Before Liana read aloud, I told the class:

Jodi: Liana was inspired by Bryan's idea to start poems in different ways. Liana's idea before our walk was to use the pattern, "I find…" as we walked. This is what she wrote.

Liana: [reads poem].

Although I don't always introduce a student, I find that it is sometimes necessary to reiterate why a student has been chosen to share.

▲▲▲▲▲▲▲▲▲▲▲▲▲▲▲

As students work through these versions of list poems, their expressions and their poems are good—but I often sense they could be better. During writing conferences I talk to children about word choice and removing words to make the poem read more smoothly. Students notice things like white space and find they can go back and revise their poems to make them stronger. As these conversations become the crux of writing conferences with most of the class, I make them whole-class explorations to take our poetry further, as I describe in the next chapter.

Taking Our Poetry Further

By the third week of our poetry unit, my students' understanding of poetry has developed far beyond their initial notion that poetry is "something that rhymes." They are beginning to see poetry as something that can take various forms. They are beginning to make connections between the poetry we read and the poetry they write. As these connections form, my students see options for taking their poetry further, moving beyond simple lists and making use of the tools other poets use to enhance their poems, such as rhythm, line breaks, and imagery. I follow their lead and expand their options to give them a bigger repertoire of tools to use in their poetry writing.

Moving Beyond Lists

One day, after modeling list poems with her class, Sue Thomas, another K/1 teacher in our school, came into my room and asked, "What do you do when your children aren't moving beyond list poems?" Sue was working on a poetry unit with her class. She mentioned that, although she thought she had explored non-list-like poems, some of her children were sticking strictly to the format of the list poems. I suggested that Sue try two things to move her students forward.

First, I recommended that she connect her list poems to special objects. Sue would ask each member of her class to bring in something special to write about the next day for poetry. This "something special" could be a picture, a seashell, a necklace, a fortune from a fortune cookie—whatever—but it had to have a special meaning to that child. Second, I suggested that Sue use her mini-lesson to model writing two poems about a special object. The first poem Sue would model would be a simple list poem. The second poem, about the same special object, would incorporate more of Sue's background knowledge of the object—where she got it, what it reminded her of, how she felt about it, etc. The key here was to tap into the range of other knowledge children could bring to their poems.

I modeled this mini-lesson for Sue to use in her class, using dinosaurs as an example:

A	B
Dinosaurs	Dinosaurs
Mean	Lived long ago
Big	Now they
Sharp teeth	are extinct.
Had babies.	They left
	Footprints
	For us
	To find.
	Footprints which
	Tell the
	Dinosaur's
	Story.

Although the poem in column A does describe dinosaurs to some extent, it doesn't tap into all of the other knowledge and impressions that a child may have about this subject. The key to moving beyond the simple list poem is introducing a way for these students to connect to the poetry that they are writing about. The poem in column B allows the child to use a list format, while incorporating her knowledge, so that the poem becomes more

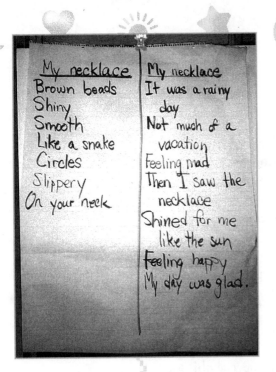

My necklace
Brown beads
Shiny
Smooth
Like a snake
Circles
Slippery
On your neck

My necklace
It was a rainy
  day
Not much of a
  vacation
Feeling mad
Then I saw the
  necklace
Shined for me
  like the sun
Feeling happy
My day was glad.

personal and distinct. Sue used special objects to try this mini-lesson and modeled writing poetry about her necklace.

Sue reported that this lesson worked well with her students. She found that modeling both kinds of poems side by side helped her students adjust their writing. This moved them beyond their list poems and encouraged them to bring more of themselves into their writing.

◄ *Sue modeled moving beyond list poems by writing a pair of poems about an important item, her necklace.*

Writing from Our Own Experiences

As the children begin to see poetry as a catch-all, a genre they could use to write about anything, they try adding new ideas to their poetry. Their experiences sneak into their poetry. The poems become less list-like and more poems that tell a story or capture a moment. The short format, the use of phrases, and the poetry paper give them the opportunity to succeed and produce many, many poems. Here is just one example of how children can capture their experiences in poetry.

My Tooth
By Philip

My tooth came out
Last night
My dad
Pulled it out
I put it
Under my
Pillow and
I saved it
And I got
20 dollars
No blood
No
Nothing
Only my
Tooth

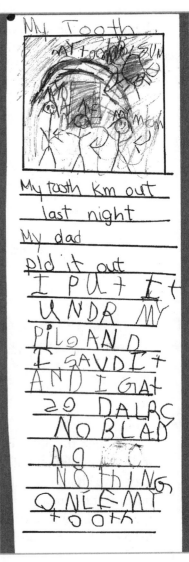

Using Short Phrases

As the children become more comfortable with their poetry writing, I often notice a lapse in the poetry form. That is, they sometimes use full sentences and long phrases, which make their poems sound more like stories. Initially, during our Paper Bag Game, we noticed that poems use short phrases. Using student work as a starting point, I present a mini-lesson around this idea so students remember to use short phrases. During one writer's workshop Isa was working on a poem about an alien toy she had.

She wrote:

> My brother gave me
> An alien toy.
> It has green eyes
> That flash and it
> Is really cool. I love that
> Green alien toy.
> It has a silver jacket too.

Isa and I talked about her poem during a writing conference.

Jodi: Isa, this poem sounds like a story to me. What could we do to make it more like a poem?

Isa: Take out some words?

Jodi: That sounds like a good start. Which words should we take out?

Isa: [taking pencil in hand and crossing out words as she talks] "It has…it is really cool…it has a…too."

Isa and I then read the newly edited poem together. I suggested to Isa that we switch the order of the last two lines so that the line "silver jacket" goes with the list of other things about the toy. I read it for her with that switch. She agreed it sounded better and went off to get a new piece of poetry paper to write her final draft. She wrote:

> My brother gave me
> An alien toy.
> Green eyes
> That flash
> Silver jacket
> I love that
> Green alien toy.

During share time, I asked Isa to talk about the revision process she used to improve her poem. She read aloud each version and we talked further about why Isa chose to take out some words and the effect it had on the "sound of the poem." Her classmates agreed that using short phrases made it sound more like poetry and less like a story. I encouraged them to try taking some words out of their poetry the next day.

The next morning when I started writer's workshop, I did a very brief mini-lesson reviewing the work that Isa had shared the day before. I asked students to look carefully at their poetry and see if they needed to take out any words. I encouraged students to read their poems out loud to their friends to make it easier to hear which phrases needed to be shortened.

This mini-lesson came directly from assessing the needs and the work of the students. Each day as I confer with my students, I assess the work that they are doing. If I see the same issue occurring with several children, I know that issue should be addressed during the share that day or the mini-lesson the next day.

"I Wonder" Poems

As children grasp that poetry can be about almost anything, I appeal to their feelings, observations, and wonderings. In one class, we had been learning about animals and I found that the children were keen observers about how animals behave, what they eat, and how they interact. Beyond animals, students were wondering about the topics we were studying. I had just returned from a trip to the Butterfly House at Callaway Gardens in Georgia, and I brought back for the children some photographs of the butterflies there. I showed the students a picture of the "Owl Butterfly." As I told my students about my trip I also started thinking aloud.

Jodi: This is one of the butterflies I saw at the Garden. It's very strange because it's called an "Owl Butterfly." Why do you think it's called that?

Kevin: Because the wings look like eyes.

Jodi: Hmm…I wonder if I could write a poem about that.

Students: Yeah, yeah…you can write about that.

I modeled writing the following poem:

Owl Butterfly

Are you a
butterfly or
are you an
owl?
You fly
like a
butterfly.
You look
like an
owl!

Jodi: When you go write today you might want to write about animals that you know about, or that you are wondering about. You are expert observers about animals. Use all of the things you know, and all of the things you are thinking about, and put them in your poems.

This poem inspired many students to write about butterflies and other animals. Samantha wrote:

> ### Monkeys
>
> Monkeys say
> Oeaahah!
> Monkeys are crazy
> Monkeys like people
> Monkeys are loud
> Monkeys.

I thought that it was very clever of Samantha to capture the sound that the monkeys make—it gave her poem such character and life—so I asked her to read it to the class. The other children loved it. We talked about how Samantha's use of that sound, which she sounded out to write, made her poem memorable.

Isa wrote about a feeling:

> ### Butterfly
>
> Once there was
> a butterfly that
> had a broken wing
> I felt bad for it
> It could only jump
> It was sort
> of raining.

Isa and I read her poem together. I asked her about the ending of her poem, which didn't seem to fit with the rest of her observations about the butterfly. Isa agreed and revised her poem, deleting the last two lines. Here again, the conference beyond the mini-lesson is an important vehicle for ensuring that the lesson sticks. In every conference I encourage students to reflect on their choice of words and to think carefully about the topics they choose.

Poems About People and Places We Love

Oftentimes during our mini-lessons we discuss writing about people and places we love. Starting one day with a family tidbit, as I usually do, I said:

Jodi: Some poets write about places they love. One of the places I love is the beach. My grandma and grandpa live on the beach in Florida. Ever since I was a little girl my family and I have been going to visit them there. I love the beach. I love the ocean. I also love walking on the beach and feeling the cool breeze in my hair and on my face. Hmm…this is starting to sound like a poem.

I began to write (having the children help me along with spelling):

The Place I love	The Place I love
Is	is
Grandma and	Grandma and
Grandpa's.	Grandpa's.
I love the beach.	I love the beach.
All	All
I see	I see
Is	is
oshn	ocean
And pam trees	and palm trees
And cokans	and coconuts
And wavs	and waves
And feel the	and feel the
Cool brez.	cool breeze.

Before I send students off to write on their own, we talk about describing meaningful people or places and the importance of including details that help others to see why they are so special to us.

Jodi: Can you think of a special place that you love?
Kevin: School.
Keiji: The park.
Rachel: New Paltz.
Will: My mom and dad's bed.
Jodi: When you go off to write today, you might want to write a poem about a place you love, or a person you love, or an animal you love. If I've inspired you to write about any of these go ahead. As always, if you are working on a different idea for a poem, that's OK too. Let's get started.

Will wrote about a place he loves:

The place I
Love is my mom
And dad's bed
Because
I can jump
On it and
Because I
Can gently
Fight with my daddy.

Max wrote his own twist about an animal he loves:

The
Animal
I love is
The rubber
Crab
Because it eats
Coconuts.

Finally, Michael wrote about a person who was special to him, his baby sister, Kaitlin.

Kaitlin
Baby
Sister
Sometimes
She
Cries
She doesn't
Cry
When
She
Sleeps.
My little sister.

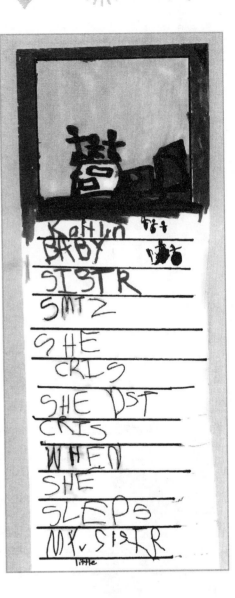

The children seemed to really understand how to write about what is important to them. They wrote about pets that had died and how they felt about losing pets or people they loved. They wrote about going special places with their families and they wrote about their friends. Whatever subject they chose, they wrote about it with care, passion, and the keen observations of a poet.

▲▲▲▲▲▲▲▲▲▲▲▲▲▲▲

Through our explorations, students learn the range of feelings and ideas they can express through poetry. They begin to fully realize what the poetry game had taught them in the very beginning of the unit—that poetry can be about anything little or big—it's how you frame it that makes it a poem. Once students reach that understanding and have the courage to write about subjects meaningful to them, I shift my focus to taking our poetry further through the use of word choice, white space, and revision.

Crafting Our Poetry

After exploring people and places we love, we begin focusing on the craft of the poetry. Poets choose their words carefully. They consider every word, and they repeat words or phrases to make a point. I want my students to craft their poems through attention to poetic elements such as repetition, word choice, and phrasing. During this focus, reading our poems aloud to each other becomes an important part of the composing process.

Using White Space

Marshall accidentally skipped a line while writing his poem one day and I pointed out that poets call that space "white space," the space they intentionally leave between lines or words. Although I hadn't planned on exploring this, I felt I needed to take Marshall's cue and use it as a "teachable moment." I pulled Marshall over to our poem of the week and asked him if he could find any "white space" there.

To his delight, he could. He pointed to the blank line between the stanzas. He felt proud of himself and we shared his findings with the class that day. The next day we revisited the white space in Marshall's poem and in our poem of the week during our mini-lesson. I suggested that other students might want to try leaving some white space and they did.

Inspired by Marshall's discovery of white space, our class began to explore other techniques that poets use to enrich their poetry. In the following mini-lessons we considered repeating poems, sound poems, and poems that connected to our school studies and outside interests.

This Tooth
By Lee Bennett Hopkins

I jiggled it
jaggled it
jerked it.

I pushed
and pulled
and poked it.

But—

As soon as I stopped,
and left it alone,
This tooth came out
on its very own!

Poems with Repetition

Furthering our study of the craft of poetry, I model repeating words to make an image or idea more powerful. During a mini-lesson I modeled writing a poem with repetition. I wrote:

Ice Cream
Sweet
Lots of flavors
Cone or dish
Lick
Lick
Lick

Then I modeled writing another poem using repetition. I wrote:

Summertime

Hot
      Hot
            Hot
Cold
   Cold
       Cold
Water
Swimming Pool.

I chose to model writing these two poems for the class because I wanted them to begin to construct their own ideas about why poets might use repetition. In addition, in the second poem, although I didn't focus on the structure of writing the words, I modeled using white space in another way, building upon our earlier discussions of white space. Our class talked about why poets might want to use repetition in their writing. The children noted that it really made the point—that saying "cold, cold, cold" meant that it was freezing! It's what we might exclaim when we jumped into cold water. During my mini-lesson, we played together with repeating words and lines. The children were already familiar with repeating the first line at the end of the poem to make it a "Circle Poem." We talked and considered which words were worth repeating. "The important ones!" the children exclaimed, and I sent them off to do just that.

Ashley began what would become a three-part poem about the beach:

Sand

Yellow	Scrunchy
Sand	Play
Sand on me	Sand
Tickle	Hot Sand
Tickle	Ouch
Tickle	Ouch
Sand built on me	Ouch
Fun	Hot Sand
Fun	Sand on me
Fun	Ouch
And more fun.	Ouch
	Ouch
	Sand
	Hot
	Hot
	And more hot.

This poem was Ashley's first attempt at using repetition in her poetry. She clearly enjoyed repeating certain words and ideas and the repetition works in this case, emphasizing the very hot temperature of the sand at the beach.

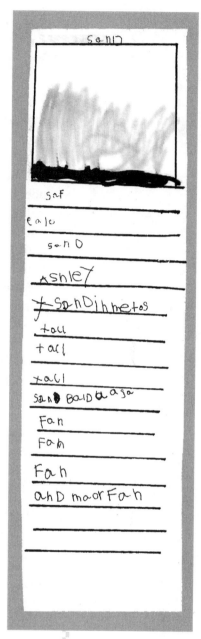

▲

Part 1 of Ashley's poem.

Sound Poems

The use of repetition in our poetry becomes even more powerful as we delve into the challenge of capturing sounds in our poems. The children begin naturally to combine their sound poems with inspirations from their repeating poems. This kind of integration, initiated by the children, shows their ownership of their writing. The children clearly begin to see themselves as poets and as the directors of the kinds of poetry they write and the ways in which they write it.

In one lesson, I asked my children, "How do you capture a sound on paper?" "How do you spell a sound?" My students had become keen observers with their eyes; now I hoped they would begin to use their ears as well. We revisited a poem of the week called "Our Washing Machine," above.

As with our study of repeating poems, we talked about why a poet might try to capture sounds in a poem. The children noted that it made it "sound like a poem," and made it more interesting. Now the task was having them get those sounds down on paper. I asked, "What kinds of things make interesting sounds that you might want to write poems about?" "Rain." "Fireworks." "Watches." "The wind." "The ocean." And they were ready to take on this new challenge. Before sending the students off to write their poems, I asked them to help me recreate some sounds on paper. I wanted to reinforce the idea that the only way to capture a sound was to use invented spelling. For some students this was not a problem. They were comfortable using invented spelling all the time. For other students, concerned about always spelling words conventionally, this was a bigger leap of faith. Yet for others, especially the struggling writers, it gave them the freedom to feel even more comfortable using invented spelling because there was no "right way" to spell a sound. Together we wrote:

"Our Washing Machine"
By Patricia Hubell

Our washing machine went whisity
    Whirr
Whisity, whisity, whisity whirr
One day at noon it went whisity click
Click grr click grr click grr click
Call the repairman
Fix it...Quick!

Waves
Woosh
Crash
Wssssssssssshhhhh.
Woosh
Crash
Wssssssssssshhhhh.
Crashing on the shore.

After our mini-lesson the students were bursting to go capture their sounds in poetry. I didn't expect so many of them to combine repetition with their sound poems, but they did.

Marshall wrote:

Trains
Chke
Chke Chke
Going down
The track
Chke chke
Chke
Trains go
Fast.

WAVS

WISH
WASH

WAVS
come
TOTHE
SHORE
SHHHH

SHHHH
WAVS

Cosmo wrote:

Waves
Wish
Wash
Waves
Come to
The shore.
Shhhhhhh.
Shhhhhhhh.
Waves.

Marshall's poem uses both repetition and sound. Cosmo's poem uses repetition and sound and is a circle poem. The combination of these elements shows both Cosmo and Marshall's understanding of how poets use these structures to create poetry.

Without even leaving our classroom, students were able to imagine sounds they wanted to include in their poems. I asked my students to continue to listen for interesting sounds as they walked to and from school and went about their daily routines. Later we could go on a poetry sound walk and listen specifically for interesting sounds to record in our poetry.

Good Books, Good Times!

by Lee Bennett Hopkins

Good books.
Good times.
Good stories.
Good rhymes.
Good beginnings.
Good ends.
Good people.
Good friends.
Good fiction.
Good facts.
Good adventures.
Good acts.
Good stories.
Good rhymes.
Good books.

Using Other Poetry Structures

Throughout our poetry unit, our poems of the week continue to serve as models for our own poetry beyond the mini-lessons I present. One week the poem of the week was Lee Bennett Hopkins' poem "Good Books, Good Times!"

Inspired by using the same word to start every line, Liana tried that structure in her writing.

Hot things.
Hot sun.
Hot classroom.
Hot neck.
Hot sweat.
Hot body
Hot chocolate
Hot volcano
Hot things.

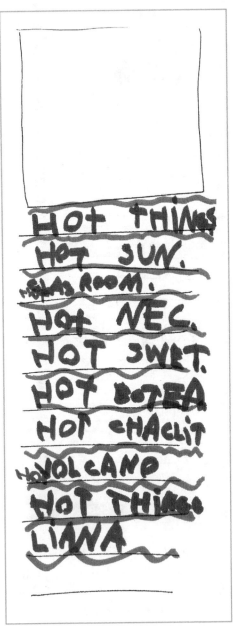

She then wrote:

Cold things.
Cold winter.
Cold ice cream.
Cold breeze.
Cold grass.
Cold hair.
Cold weather.
Cold water.
Cold things.

Liana used both the idea of using a repeating first word and Lee Bennett Hopkins' circle poem structure to create her poem.

▲▲▲▲▲▲▲▲▲▲▲▲▲▲

Through the mini-lessons and class writing shares, our poetry prospers. One year, simultaneously, my class was working on a science unit on "How Things Are Made." Their research and understanding about how things work began to creep into their poetry, demonstrating that poetry truly links to all curriculum areas, a topic I address in the next chapter.

COLD THINGS.
COLD WINTR.
COLD ICE CREAM.
COLD BRES.
COLD GRAS.
COLD HAR.
COLD WETHR
COLD WATR
COLD THINGS
Liana
LIANA
Liana
LIANA
Liana

Linking Poetry to the Curriculum

During the spring of 2000, I was asked to speak about poetry at a conference focusing on Mathematics and Science at Kean University in New Jersey. I was initially apprehensive about connecting poetry to science and wondered how these two curriculum areas would mesh. I soon realized that science and literacy are linked continuously in our school lives. Scientists are similar to poets in many respects. For example, in the Paper Bag Game that introduces our poetry unit, we focus

on characteristics of items—
describing them, classifying
them, and recording our
thoughts. I ask my students to
look closely and give clues about
each object. In doing so, they
observe with all their senses,
using their previous knowledge
about these objects to give clues
and help others make guesses.
The poets in my classroom *were*
scientists! And so I began to
compile their similarities:

Scientists	Poets
☼ OBSERVE	☼ OBSERVE
☼ GATHER	☼ GATHER (ideas, thoughts)
☼ RECORD (data)	☼ RECORD (happenings, thoughts)
☼ NOTICE	☼ NOTICE
☼ HYPOTHESIZE	☼ WONDER
☼ EXPERIMENT	☼ EXPERIMENT (w/language, structure)
☼ CONCLUDE	☼ CONCLUDE

Linking Poetry and Science

At the same time my class was engaged in our poetry study, we were
also working on a science unit about "How Things are Made." Each
child was responsible for finding out how something was made or
worked and then presenting their research (with a family member's help) to
the class. Some students also provided an activity for the class. At the end of
the unit we made a class museum, "T.M.H.T.M." (The Museum of How
Things are Made). Each child was an expert on her topic, which ranged from
the natural, such as icicles, rainbows, and volcanoes; to the biological, such as
how butterflies, frogs, and silk are made; to the arts,
such as how candles and paper bag dragons are made.
The presentations were fascinating and the children
certainly were experts. I wasn't sure, however, how
much information the rest of the class was absorbing—
that is, until writing workshop rolled around.

After a few weeks of mini-lessons the children were
feeling comfortable in finding topics to write about
for their poems. Cosmo had just given a presentation
on jelly beans and during writing workshop he wrote:

Sweet

Have
Lots of
Colors
Jelly Beans

I was impressed that Cosmo felt confident enough as a poet to capture his expertise on jelly beans in a poem. Eli had recently done a presentation on how icicles are made. He even packed some icicles from his house and brought them in for us to touch and hold. Emily was inspired by Eli's presentation and wrote:

Icicles

Melt
Cold
You can play
with them
Wet
Melt
When it is hot
Icicles

After reading Emily's poem, I thought, Wow, these kids really are acting and writing like poets. They are using their newly acquired knowledge as inspiration for their writing. Not only were they learning about crafting poems, but they were absorbing a great deal of information from the presentations of their peers. Their poems provided a wonderful way for me to assess their comprehension.

Declan gave a presentation on volcanoes with his father. Agim, a struggling writer, was so inspired he wanted to write a poem about Declan's presentation. With help from a student teacher Agim wrote:

Volcanoes

Lava
Fire
Erupts

Agim usually has trouble getting started with writing, but on this day he was inspired, and from then on he was excited that he could write about the presentations classmates gave each day.

Emily and her mother presented on how rainbows are formed and included an activity that described the order of the colors and their names. After Emily's presentation Rennick wrote:

Rainbows

They have
Pretty colors
They have
Nice pretty
Bright colors
They go in
Order
Beautiful rainbows.

I was pleasantly surprised that our science curriculum was finding its way into our writing. The children were teaching me about integrating the curriculum! I then looked back at some of the poems children created at the beginning of the unit with a partner. When we returned from the zoo and animals were on our minds, many children chose to write about animals. Vinny and Will wrote:

Gorillas

Strong
Live in the jungle
Used to be human
Beings
Have
Babies
Gorillas

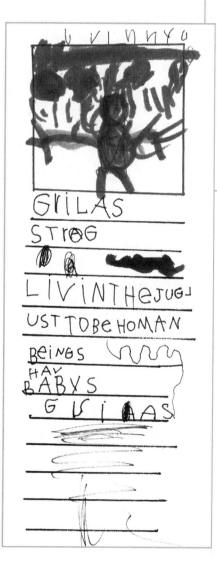

Wow! These kids were going beyond describing the characteristics of an animal; they were describing its habitat and even pondering its role in evolution! As I looked back at their work in the new light of seeing them as poet-scientists, my initial thoughts about the connection between the two were affirmed.

Another partnership created this poem:

Cats

Eyes glow
In the dark
Last for
20 years
Sharp claws
Purr
Meow
Tails go swish
When they are mad
Cats

Later in the year, after I had finished my poetry unit, Sue Thomas, another K/1 teacher, began hers. At the same time, Sue's class was studying ants. Her room housed five ant farms, and Sue had asked children to write down observations of the ants in their farms. When I went to visit Sue's class, she showed me the wonderful observations children had made. As she read them to me we agreed that they sounded like poems. Sue decided that after exploring poetry further with her children, she would return to these observations and use them as inspirations for a class book of ant poems. One child wrote "The ants dig the sand and take the sand to the top of the sand. The ants eye is like a pensol dot." Another child wrote, "They ant[s] are crawl. The ant. The ant are [marching] by one. The ant go mrching." Sue's kids, too, were scientist-poets. The connection was once again made by these amazing observers, who are capable of simultaneously recording their poetic and scientific thoughts.

Independent Poetry Writing Projects

As the poetry unit progresses, my mini-lessons become even more abbreviated, and the poetry that students produce begins to take on a life of its own. My students truly become poets. They sit down to write one-, two-, and three-part poems. They make books of their own poems. Logan, inspired by the monthly pattern calendars on our wall, decided to write a book of poems about the months of the year.

Isa, an animal lover, chose to write a collection of poems about animals. Each day, Isa added two, three, or four poems to her collection. Other students, encouraged by Isa and Logan's work, decided to make collections of poems during writing time. They understood that the poems should be bound together by a common theme. Julia and Liana crafted poems about animals. Isa created her own form for her poetry using a pattern and theme to connect her poems. Her work incorporated all of the elements of poetry that we had explored together as well as other elements Isa had gleaned through reading lots of poetry on her own and with her family.

As you read through Isa's poems you see the evolution of her own understandings of how poetry should look, feel, and sound. In addition, although we didn't explore rhyming poems together in class, Isa uses rhyme well. She clearly worked as a poet would, by choosing her words carefully. The following are some of Isa's poems.

Poodles

Poodles are
Very pretty
When they
Walk they
Are very
Sitty. When
They bark
They sound
Very
Frightening, but they're still pretty.

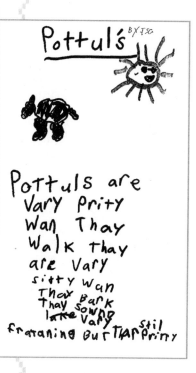

Pottuls'

Pottuls are
Vary Prity
Wan Thay
Walk thay
are Vary
sitty wan
Thay Bark
Thay sowng
lare Vary
fraraning Bur TIAP Prity stil

turttels

Tanttels
are vary
slou and arevBaty
kno's Thar Tirttes
ovisiy Dont ware
Bo's!

Turtles

Turtles
Are very
Slow and everybody
Knows that turtles
Obviously don't wear
Bows.

Snak's
BY Isa

Snak's are
vary slithrry!
wan they Move
You are scamp
Thay one naver
averParb, you naver
Have a snak for
A Pat!

Snakes

Snakes are
Very slithery!
When they move
You are scared.
They are never
Ever paired.
You never
Have a snake for a pet!

Begils

Begils are vary
loing I naver Herd
orThaT of A Begil
Song?? and Becose
Thêre so loing
I call Tham
A
Hot Dog!?!

Beagles

Beagles are very
Long. I never heard
Of a beagle
Song. And because
They're so long
I call them
A
Hot Dog!

The students' independent projects were further indications that they had truly internalized the work we had done together on poetry. They understood that poetry was everywhere and that poetry could take on many forms. In addition, they were free to experiment with language as poets do. This was more than I had hoped for.

▲▲▲▲▲▲▲▲▲▲▲▲

Sharing Our Work Daily

Beyond talking about animals and things we observe, we share our writing every day. We share strategies, ideas for poems, and ways to use descriptive language. We celebrate each poem. Some days, elated by the work the children produce, I type it up and send it home in their mailboxes. I cannot contain the enthusiasm and success that fills our classroom during writing time. Students can't wait to take their poetry home. Parents arrive each morning praising the poetry their children have written. With all this excitement I realize that it's time to have a formal celebration of all of our hard work.

Celebrating Our Poetry

When the children and I decide it's time for a more formal celebration of our poetry, the excitement mounts. We plan a Poetry Reading; we invite family and caregivers into our classroom to listen to and enjoy the poems we have created. Students eagerly revisit their work, polishing the poems to make them the best they can be. For some children it means adding more details to their pictures; for others it means fixing the spelling of words they know. To help students get their poems ready for publication, I guide them through editing and revision conferences with peers and teachers.

Editing Conferences

At the end of our poetry unit, I ask students to choose two poems they would like to share at our Poetry Reading. Usually I ask children to "publish" all of their poems, but only share two aloud at the reading. Children revise these poems and edit them for conventional spelling.

I have taken two different approaches to publishing student work. One year I simply typed all the poems children had written and glued them, four to a page, onto large construction paper. I also typed translations of each poem and glued it next to the original. I then laminated the poems and joined pages with a metal ring. At the Poetry Reading, each child read from his own collection of poems.

Another year I took the publishing process a step further. I asked the children to pick one poem that they would like to share at our reading. The rest of their poems were mounted and published in the aforementioned manner. The poem of their choice, however, I made into a book of its own. I had shared many poetry books with the students during our unit, several of which were collections of poetry. Some were picture books with one poem narrating a story. We revisited these books, and I told students that we too would turn our poems into books of their own. This was a lengthy process and took place over a week or so.

First, the students chose the poem they wanted to publish. I had them read aloud their poems with partners and decide on any revisions they wanted to make. When all revisions were made, I conferred with each child and helped him find the conventional spelling for any misspelled words.

As Rachel read her poems aloud, she crossed out the words that didn't make sense.

Revision

During my writing conferences I have the children read their poems aloud to me. As they read, I point to the words they have written. Often, a child will have skipped a word, or added an extra word and, together, we discover the mistake. As Rachel read me the poems at left, she discovered that she had added extra words that didn't make sense. Rachel decided to edit them out. I showed Rachel how to strike through a word on her first poem. As we read the second poem together, she did it on her own.

Rennick's poem on crayons was pretty basic. I knew that Rennick was capable of writing more and therefore pushed him to add to his simple poem about crayons. Rennick's first draft read:

Crayons

Colors
Red
Blue
Dark Pink
Orange
Green
Black
Crayons

I gave Rennick an initial suggestion for describing those colors.

Jodi: Red like what? Green like what? How can you help me see those colors in my mind?

Rennick: Red like an apple?

Jodi: Yes. Write that. What else?

Rennick: Blue like the sky.

Jodi: You got it…can you do that for each color?

Rennick continued working on his poem and his final poem read:

Crayons

Colors
Red like an apple
Blue like the sky
Dark pink like cotton candy
Orange like an orange
Green like grass
Black like the night
Purple like grapes
Yellow like the sun
Pink like valentines
Crayons

Rennick's revisions made his poem even more effective. I pushed Rennick to make these refinements because he was a fluent and passionate writer who hesitated to stretch himself to do his best. I probably wouldn't have suggested such revisions for a very emergent writer. As a teacher, you feel what's right for each student, nudge him, and offer support in the way that is most effective for his own development.

This revision work is not usually followed up with a second draft of the poem. The only time I ask some of my students to do second drafts is for their final published pieces. Even then, if their work is fairly neat and legible, I honor their initial work and do not ask them to rewrite their poems, although they are free to do so if they want.

Publishing: Final Touches

Having revised and edited their work, the students have the opportunity to prepare a final draft of their poems. This done, students work with a parent volunteer to make accordion books for their poems. After they make their books, I cut their poems apart along the line breaks and glue them into their accordion books. Accordion books fold out like accordions: All the pages are connected at the seams so that the book can be stretched out and all the text and illustrations viewed at once. I like this format because it honors the integrity of the poem while mapping that form onto an illustrated book. I also glue in a complete typed copy of the poem. After their words are in their books, students complete the illustrations for each line of their poem. The accordion book structure allows the poems to feel like a book and, at the same time, remain a continuous piece of writing. When the books are done, we are ready to celebrate!

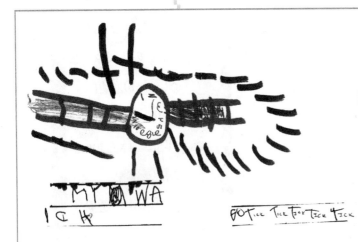

Vinny made his poem into a picture book.

▲▲▲▲▲▲▲▲▲▲▲▲▲

Celebrating Our Work

Children make invitations to the poetry reading and all parents are invited to join us. The reading is followed by a class breakfast. The children read, and each is applauded in celebration of her success. Each and every child reads poems written from the heart. And each and every child's progress is reflected in the work shared.

I had set a goal for my students—getting more letters, sounds, and words on paper. I knew they were articulate, but they didn't seem as free in their writing. Our poetry study gave them a short, sweet way to try their skills at getting words and letters down on paper. The short format of the poem gave the children a task they knew they could accomplish in a limited amount of time. Rather than writing a story, which may take days, a child could whip off a poem or even two in a writing session.

Young children are still very egocentric. All their thoughts and observations are important to them. They are naturally astute observers of their own lives and their own thinking. Therefore, having them pick one small nugget, such as a special place, person, or even an understanding about an animal, allowed them to choose from the plethora of thoughts swirling in their heads. Using these ideas for poetry gave them a valid place where they could be expressed.

Recently, a few months after concluding our poetry unit, I was introducing a new poem for the week, "Nature is Very Busy." We had been growing caterpillars into butterflies in our classroom, and this poem seemed appropriate. Together we explored it:

Nature Is Very Busy

By Frances Gorman Risser

Bees are buzzing, frogs are hopping,
Moles are digging. There's no stopping
Vines from climbing, grass from growing,
Birds from singing, winds from blowing,
Buds from blooming, crickets humming,
Sunbeams dancing, raindrops drumming.
All the world is whirling, dizzy
Nature is very busy!

After reading this poem three times, Marshall raised his hand and said, "Hey, that's a circle poem—it starts and ends the same way!" Wow! I hadn't even thought of that! I had picked this poem for its connection to our curriculum, not for a model of poetry. Then Eli commented, "It's a list poem, too. It lists things that happen in nature." Another wow! These kids had gotten it. They had become experts on circle and list poems. Isa chimed in, "It's also a sound poem. It captures a lot of sounds in nature." Rennick added, "It's also a rhyming poem." And so the conversation went as we talked about all of the things we knew about this kind of poem. I was impressed. These students saw poetry around them. Their conversations were evidence that they had indeed become successful, confident, independent poets.

Name:

Date:

Name:

Date:

Joyful Ways to Teach Young Children to Write Poetry
Scholastic Professional Books

Joyful Ways to Teach Young Children to Write Poetry
Scholastic Professional Books